A Self Help Book for Christian Teen Girls

CRAFTED BY SKRIUWER

Copyright © 2024 by Skriuwer.

All rights reserved. No part of this book may be used or reproduced in any form whatsoever without written permission except in the case of brief quotations in critical articles or reviews.

For more information, contact : **kontakt@skriuwer.com** (www.skriuwer.com)

TABLE OF CONTENTS

CHAPTER 1: UNDERSTANDING YOUR WORTH

- Recognizing that true value comes from God, not social approval
- Learning to see yourself through a biblical lens
- Practical steps to guard against comparison and insecurity

CHAPTER 2: BUILDING A STRONG FOUNDATION

- The importance of biblical truths as a base for life
- Developing moral guidelines and personal discipline
- Forming healthy habits that support long-term stability

CHAPTER 3: MANAGING STRESS AND WORRY

- Identifying causes of anxiety and practical ways to reduce it
- Finding comfort in prayer and Scripture during tense moments
- Tips for keeping a positive mindset and healthier routines

CHAPTER 4: MAKING HEALTHY FRIENDSHIPS

- Qualities that define supportive, godly friendships
- Establishing boundaries, resolving conflicts, and building trust
- Encouraging kindness and respect among peers

CHAPTER 5: HANDLING SOCIAL MEDIA AND TECHNOLOGY

- Setting wise boundaries for digital consumption
- Avoiding negative comparisons and toxic content online
- Using technology for growth, service, and faith-based connections

CHAPTER 6: STANDING UP FOR YOUR VALUES

- Learning to say "no" with courage and conviction
- Handling peer pressure and ridicule without losing faith
- Balancing humility and boldness in moral choices

CHAPTER 7: GROWING THROUGH HARD TIMES

- Trusting God's presence during trials and grief
- Finding encouragement from Scripture and supportive mentors
- Turning pain into empathy and strength

CHAPTER 8: FINDING STRENGTH IN PRAYER

- Building a daily prayer routine that nurtures intimacy with God
- Different types of prayer (praise, confession, thanksgiving, requests)
- Overcoming common struggles and distractions in prayer

CHAPTER 9: EXPLORING POSITIVE HABITS

- Identifying and replacing harmful habits with constructive ones
- Practical tips for self-discipline, accountability, and balance
- Using good routines to shape mind, body, and spirit

CHAPTER 10: BUILDING STRONG FAMILY CONNECTIONS

- Showing respect, love, and genuine care within the home
- Handling conflicts with patience, forgiveness, and honest talk
- Serving, supporting, and growing together as a family unit

CHAPTER 11: STAYING PURE IN HEART AND MIND

- Guarding thoughts, media intake, and personal boundaries
- Understanding purity beyond physical actions—focusing on motives
- Overcoming temptations through Scripture, prayer, and accountability

CHAPTER 12: BECOMING A LEADER AT SCHOOL & CHURCH

- Traits of a servant leader who inspires others
- Balancing confidence with humility and integrity
- Handling criticism, guiding teams, and standing out for Christ

CHAPTER 13: HANDLING DOUBTS AND QUESTIONS

- Approaching faith struggles honestly rather than ignoring them
- Strategies for finding answers through mentors, Scripture, and prayer
- Staying committed to God's truth despite lingering uncertainties

CHAPTER 14: USING GIFTS AND TALENTS WISELY

- Recognizing your unique abilities and developing them
- Avoiding pride or comparison while serving God and others
- Combining skills with compassion to make a lasting impact

CHAPTER 15: DEVELOPING SELF-CONTROL

- Identifying triggers that lead to impulsive decisions or anger
- Setting personal guidelines, using accountability, and trusting God
- Balancing healthy emotions while pursuing self-discipline

CHAPTER 16: HELPING OTHERS IN THE COMMUNITY

- Finding local needs and volunteering effectively
- Organizing group projects, supporting the homeless or elderly
- Blending practical service with a Christlike attitude

CHAPTER 17: LEARNING FROM ROLE MODELS

- Spotting positive influences—biblical, historical, modern
- Filtering out unhealthy or misleading examples
- Becoming a role model yourself for younger individuals

CHAPTER 18: SETTING GOALS WITH FAITH

- Aligning personal aspirations with biblical principles
- Using the S.M.A.R.T. approach alongside prayer and surrender
- Staying motivated, flexible, and God-centered in your planning

CHAPTER 19: BUILDING A BRIGHT FUTURE

- Embracing greater independence and responsibility
- Gaining practical life skills, including budgeting and time management
- Maintaining an eternal perspective while pursuing career or academic goals

CHAPTER 20: TRUSTING GOD IN ALL AREAS OF LIFE

- Letting faith guide your emotions, relationships, and future plans
- Finding peace in unanswered prayers and challenging circumstances
- Living daily in surrender, secure in God's unwavering love and care

CHAPTER 1

Understanding Your Worth

Introduction
Many teenage girls feel unsure of themselves at times. They see other people on social media or in real life who seem to have everything together. It might make them question their own value. At times, you might wonder if you measure up to the expectations of your friends, family, and even your church community. But it is important to know that your worth does not rely on how you look, what you wear, or who you hang out with. Your worth comes from your identity as a child of God.

The Bible says in Psalm 139:14 that we are all "wonderfully made." This means you are not an accident. God made you with great care. This fact alone should encourage you. While the world might make you feel like you need to compete or compare yourself with others, God sees you as valuable from the start.

Below are some deeper insights that go beyond common tips you may hear. These points are meant to help you see yourself through God's eyes. Taking time to truly understand them will help you feel confident, even when others do not see your true value.

---

1. Knowing Where True Value Comes From

One idea that is easy to miss is the difference between worth and approval from others. Many teens measure their success by the number of "likes" they get on social media or whether they have the latest trends. However, true value does not come from such things. True value does not decrease just because your outfit is not brand-name, or because you are not the most popular girl in school.

- **God as the Source of Your Worth**
  Human approval is not steady. Sometimes, people like you. Other times, they might overlook you. God's view, on the other hand, does not change. The Bible reminds us that nothing can separate us from the love of God. That means your worth is attached to a source that does not run out or fade.
- **A Practical Example**
  Think about a precious coin or a rare stamp. Its value remains, even if

people do not notice it. People might not always recognize the worth of that item, but it does not stop being special. In the same way, your worth is set by the One who made you, not by those who glance your way.

2. Why Insecurities Grow

To understand your worth, you must also see why you might feel insecure. Some reasons could be:

- **Comparisons in Daily Life**: You see someone with perfect hair or a perfect figure, and you think you need to be like them to be valuable.
- **Harsh Criticism**: Maybe you have heard negative words from friends or even family members. Such words can linger in your mind and make you doubt yourself.
- **Fear of Failing**: Sometimes, you might worry that if you fail a test or do poorly in sports, it means you are not good enough in general.

None of these should define who you are. Rather, you should look for deeper truths about your life.

A Lesser-Known Tip: In a modern world, many people say, "Stop comparing yourself." But that can be hard to do without something stronger to lean on. Instead, try changing your view: see each person as created by God with unique gifts. When you realize that your friend or classmate was made by the same God, you can appreciate them without feeling less about yourself. This helps lessen that urge to compare.

3. Practical Steps to Embrace Your God-Given Value

Though we are avoiding certain words, we can use direct actions that support a positive mindset:

1. **Quiet Reflection Time**: Spend a few minutes every day thinking about how God sees you. This can be as simple as sitting quietly and reminding yourself, "I am precious in God's sight. My worth is beyond numbers or opinions."
2. **Daily Affirmations from Scripture**: Write down verses like Luke 12:7 ("Even the hairs on your head are all numbered") or Ephesians 2:10 ("We

are God's handiwork"). Put them in places you see often. Repeating these truths can help you believe them on a deeper level.
3. **Choose Encouraging Friends**: Seek friendships with those who respect you and see your true value. You become stronger in faith when you are around people who also believe in God's love and plan for your life.
4. **Participate in Meaningful Activities**: Find ways to use the talents God gave you. Whether it is singing in your church's choir, helping younger kids with homework, or learning an instrument, engaging in tasks that match your gifts can remind you that you have a special purpose.

---

4. Guarding Against Outside Influences

The world is full of messages that might make you feel unworthy. Advertisements, social media, and even peers can send subtle suggestions that you need something extra to be acceptable. Here are ways to protect yourself:

- **Wise Media Consumption**: Before you buy into the message of an ad or a show, ask yourself if it aligns with godly truths. Does it push you to chase appearances, or does it guide you toward developing good qualities?
- **Limit Negative Inputs**: If certain songs, movies, or social media accounts make you feel terrible about who you are, it is okay to step back. You can choose what enters your mind and heart.
- **Stay Mindful of Gossip**: Sometimes, classmates gossip or judge people's looks or status. Recognize that these conversations rarely match God's view of you. If possible, walk away or politely change the topic.

---

5. Understanding God's Creation Beyond Surface Details

Many people talk about "loving yourself," but fail to mention the deeper reason: God made you. Accepting this truth is more powerful than any self-help catchphrase. Remember that God created not just your body, but also your mind and soul. You are intricate, and your value extends beyond simple traits:

- **Your Mind**: Your ability to think, learn, and create ideas is a gift. Using your mind to study Scripture, discover new hobbies, or help others is a way to honor God.
- **Your Body**: Health is important, but do not stress about unrealistic standards. Show respect to your body by eating balanced meals, staying

active, and avoiding harmful substances. That kind of care is a form of gratitude.
- **Your Soul**: This is the eternal part of you. When you feel anxious or alone, remember that your soul is connected to God in a deep way. Spending time with Him in prayer or Bible study can calm your mind and remind you of your lasting worth.

---

6. Unique Strengths That Show Your Value

Young people often overlook hidden talents. For instance, you might be very good at listening to friends or you might have a knack for fixing problems at home. These might not always be rewarded in public, but they are special. Look for qualities that seem small yet make a big difference in someone's life. God has placed these strengths in you for a purpose.

A Rare Tip: Try a mini-experiment for self-discovery. Pick one day of the week when you intentionally try out a new positive behavior. For example, decide to compliment three people about something sincere. Notice how it feels. Or decide to ask a teacher about a volunteer role you can fill at school. This can help you see talents you never noticed before.

---

7. Handling Doubt About Your Worth

Even when you know you are precious to God, doubt can sneak in. Perhaps you mess up, or someone criticizes you. Doubt is normal, but it does not have to rule your life.

- **The Power of Asking Questions**: Instead of letting doubt spiral, ask questions like, "Is this feeling based on truth?" or "Does God still say I am valuable?" This allows you to pause and refocus on what is real.
- **Seek Support**: Talking to a trusted adult or spiritual mentor can help. Find someone who is mature in faith and share your feelings openly. They can often guide you back to a healthier perspective.

8. Building a Lifestyle Around Your Worth

Knowing your worth is not just an idea. It changes how you live day by day. Here are specific habits to form:

1. **Speak Kindly About Yourself**: Use respectful words when talking about your looks and abilities. If you catch yourself saying negative things about your body or your intelligence, stop and rephrase them into something kinder.
2. **Stand Firm in Your Beliefs**: If you hold to Christian principles, do not hide them just to fit in. Your values are part of your identity. Being confident in them shows that you know you have nothing to prove to the crowd.
3. **Keep Growing Spiritually**: Spend time reading your Bible or devotionals. This constant input of truth keeps you grounded and confident. Many teens read a chapter of Proverbs daily or use a Bible app plan to stay consistent.
4. **Surround Yourself With Positive Environments**: Churches, youth groups, and school clubs that share your morals can strengthen your sense of self-worth. These groups support your growth instead of tearing you down.

---

9. Preventing an Inflated Ego

One challenge is striking a balance between healthy confidence and arrogance. You are created with purpose, and you are special to God, but that does not mean you are better than anyone else. Arrogance can hurt friendships and push people away.

- **Humility as a Strength**: Jesus displayed humility even though He is the Son of God. He washed His disciples' feet (John 13:1-17). Remembering this helps you stay grateful rather than looking down on others.
- **Focus on Service**: One way to keep your confidence in check is by serving people who have needs. You can volunteer at your church or help a lonely friend. When you show kindness, it reminds you that worth is about reflecting God's love, not bragging about yourself.

10. Reflecting on Mistakes Without Losing Self-Worth

You will make mistakes at times. That is part of being human. Instead of seeing these moments as proof that you are worthless, think of them as opportunities to learn.

- **Separate Action from Identity**: You might fail a test, but that does not make you a failure as a person. You might say something mean to a sibling, but that does not make you permanently unkind. Recognize your actions but remain aware that your identity as God's child does not shift.
- **Seek Forgiveness**: If your mistake involves hurting someone, apologize and make efforts to repair the relationship. This teaches you responsibility and shows that you respect yourself and others enough to make things right.
- **Learn and Move Forward**: Instead of dwelling on the error, figure out what caused it, plan how to avoid it next time, and then carry on. This approach keeps your self-worth strong.

---

11. Common Misunderstandings About Self-Worth

Several myths can lead teens astray:

- **Myth: Confidence Means Being Loud or Popular**
  You can be quiet and still be sure of yourself. Confidence means trusting that God's design for you is enough.
- **Myth: Academic or Athletic Success Determines Worth**
  Achievements can be good, but they do not create or destroy your value. They are only add-ons.
- **Myth: You Have to Prove Your Worth**
  In reality, God has already settled the question of your worth. You do not have to prove yourself through likes or trophies.

---

12. Using Your Worth to Influence Others Positively

When you understand that you are valuable, you can inspire others to see their own value. You might be the one who greets the new student at school or stands up against bullying. When your identity is secure, you can give support to friends who struggle.

Advanced Thought: People often follow those who act with true confidence. You do not need to be the loudest person. Steady kindness and faith can draw people in more than flashy behavior. By simply treating people well and staying firm in who you are, you become a positive role model.

---

13. Tying It All Together

Your worth is fixed because God has named you His child. It cannot be undone by outside opinions, temporary failures, or changing trends. To truly believe this, you need to keep reminding yourself of biblical truths, surround yourself with healthy influences, and look for ways to use your gifts for good.

Questions for Personal Reflection

1. In what moments do you feel most unsure about your worth?
2. Which Bible verse gives you the greatest encouragement about your value?
3. How can you use your talents to show love to others?

Practical Action Point
Pick one person in your life—maybe a classmate who is often left out—and offer a genuine compliment or act of kindness. Then pay attention to how this makes you feel about yourself. By lifting someone else up, you often grow in personal confidence as well.

Conclusion to Chapter 1
Understanding your worth is a foundational step. Once you see yourself the way God does, you can handle everyday life challenges from a position of strength rather than insecurity. You can form healthier relationships, set stronger boundaries, and use your gifts in the world. This mindset will play a major role in how you read and apply the lessons in the chapters that follow.

CHAPTER 2

Building a Strong Foundation

Introduction

A building is only as sturdy as the ground under it. In the same way, your beliefs, values, and daily habits form the base of your life. A shaky foundation makes it easier for fears, doubts, and negative influences to bring you down. But a strong one keeps you steady, even when problems come your way.

In this chapter, we will look at how to build a lasting foundation that supports a healthy and faithful life. This includes spiritual practices, moral guidelines, and personal discipline. Rather than giving you surface-level pointers, we will focus on deeper methods that many teens overlook. By applying these methods, you will be better able to stick to your Christian values and handle any challenges that pop up.

---

1. Why a Strong Foundation Matters

People sometimes ignore the importance of developing a stable internal base. They might think that as long as they avoid big mistakes, they are fine. However, a sturdy foundation is what keeps you grounded when you face peer pressure, disappointment, or unexpected problems. Think of this foundation as the core set of beliefs and habits that define you:

- **Acts as a Guiding Compass**: When you are not sure what choice to make, your foundation in faith helps you find the right path.
- **Provides Emotional Security**: Knowing that you stand on firm ground can reduce stress. You are not easily swayed by opinions or rude comments.
- **Nourishes Growth**: With a stable base, you can learn new things and build relationships without losing sight of who you really are.

---

2. Building on Biblical Truth

Your belief system should come from a trustworthy source. For Christians, the Bible is that source. By regularly reading it, you learn about God's nature, promises, and expectations. However, there is more to the Bible than just popular stories:

- **Exploring the Full Context**: Try reading not just your favorite passages but also the introductions, historical notes, and cross-references. This will help you see the bigger picture.
- **Applying the Lessons**: When the Bible says, "Love your neighbor," it is not just an idea. It calls for actions such as showing kindness, forgiving wrongs, and helping those in need.
- **Memorizing Key Verses**: Pick verses that speak directly to your life. Repeat them until you can recall them during tough moments. This hidden store of truth will guide your thoughts.

An Advanced Tip: Instead of random reading, follow a structured reading plan that covers different books in an organized way. For example, read a chapter of Proverbs for wisdom, then read part of the Gospels to learn from Jesus's teachings, and then explore a Psalm for encouragement. This balanced approach gives you a broader understanding.

---

3. Setting Moral Guidelines

Many teens think rules are just there to limit fun. But moral guidelines based on Christian teachings are there to protect and help you. They act like guardrails on a winding road, keeping you from going off track.

- **Deciding on Boundaries Early**: Before you face a tricky situation, figure out your limits. For example, decide how far is too far in a dating relationship or whether you will attend parties with underage drinking.
- **Standing Firm on Standards**: If friends try to push you to do something against your beliefs, remember that you set these standards for a reason. You are not being rude by saying no; you are respecting your own convictions.
- **Being Honest with Yourself**: Understand your personal weak spots. If you know you are easily influenced in certain areas, set stricter boundaries for yourself. This is not a sign of weakness but a sign of wisdom.

---

4. Developing Personal Discipline

Personal discipline means controlling your actions, thoughts, and words. It is not only about big moral decisions; it also includes everyday habits. Here are effective ways to improve your discipline:

- **Regular Prayer**: Talking to God daily keeps your focus on Him. If you only pray when you need something, you miss out on a consistent connection that can shape your character.
- **Planned Schedule**: A simple plan for your day can reduce wasted time and keep you on track. Decide when you will do homework, when you will pray, and when you will rest.
- **Accountability**: Find a friend or mentor you trust to hold you responsible. Share your goals with them, and ask for a gentle check-in to make sure you are following through.

---

5. The Role of Christian Community

Being part of a healthy Christian community is a key factor in building a strong foundation. This could be your church youth group, a Bible study club at school, or an online Christian forum. The main point is that you need fellowship with other believers who will encourage you to grow.

- **Learning from Shared Wisdom**: In a group, you can hear how others overcame the same challenges you are facing. Their experience can save you from making similar mistakes.
- **Opportunities for Service**: Many churches or Christian groups plan community outreach or mission trips. Joining these helps you exercise your faith and develop compassion for others.
- **Building Supportive Relationships**: A Christian friend can comfort you and pray with you when you go through difficulties. Having someone who shares your faith can make a huge difference in your day-to-day walk.

---

6. Healthy Habits that Strengthen Your Base

Along with spiritual practices, everyday habits play a part in making you strong. Teenagers sometimes overlook things like nutrition, sleep, and mental focus, but these are vital.

- **Good Eating and Exercise**: A well-cared-for body helps you feel more energetic and focused. That energy can translate into better attention during prayer and Bible study.
- **Stress Management**: Methods like writing in a journal or taking short breaks during study sessions can keep stress from piling up. Too much stress can weaken your resolve.
- **Respecting Rest**: Always getting less sleep than you need can make you more likely to snap at others, skip your devotions, or let your mind wander in church. Prioritizing rest is a wise choice.

Seldom Discussed Insight: Some studies show that teens who get enough sleep handle emotional stresses better and even do better academically. This can help you remain consistent in your faith-based decisions, because exhaustion often leads to impulsive or careless actions.

---

7. Leading Yourself Before Leading Others

Teens often look for leadership roles in school clubs, sports teams, or church groups. Good leadership starts with leading yourself well. If you cannot practice discipline, patience, and kindness in your own life, you will struggle to guide others.

- **Stay True to Your Beliefs**: Leadership is about setting an example. If you cut corners, others will notice.
- **Be Open to Learning**: Even as a leader, you are still growing. Accept advice from those with more experience.
- **Reflect on Actions Regularly**: Once a week, think about how you handled your responsibilities. Did you show fairness, respect, and integrity?

Deep Thought: People respect leaders who live their morals consistently. If you are the same person in private and in public, you build trust. Remember that every leader in the Bible who did great things also spent time alone with God, checking their hearts and motives.

---

8. Tackling Common Struggles with a Strong Base

Even with a firm foundation, struggles will appear. The difference is that you will have the tools to handle them. Here are some common areas where a strong base is beneficial:

1. **Dealing with Peer Pressure**: When classmates encourage risky behavior, your prepared moral guidelines keep you from giving in.
2. **Facing Disappointment**: If you fail at something, your identity is not ruined because your value does not come from achievements.
3. **Handling Fear**: Anxiety can be calmed by prayer, reflection on Scripture, and conversations with a mentor.

9. How to Maintain Stability When Life Changes

Changes are part of the teenage years: moving schools, watching friendships shift, or seeing family dynamics evolve. These changes can test your foundation if you are unprepared.

- **Regular Check-Ups**: Every few months, evaluate your spiritual habits, friendships, and daily routines. Make adjustments as needed.
- **Stay Connected to Mentors**: Keeping open communication with a youth leader, pastor, or parent can help you sort through transitions.
- **Adapt Without Compromising**: Some changes are good, like starting a new extracurricular activity. Just be sure it does not clash with your moral guidelines or take you away from important spiritual routines.

10. Influencing Others to Build Foundations

Once you start seeing the benefits of a strong foundation, you might want to share these with friends. Some may not be open to Christian beliefs, but you can still share universal principles like kindness, honesty, and discipline.

- **Speak About What Works for You**: Instead of preaching at people, talk about specific ways your habits or faith have helped you.
- **Offer Help**: If a friend is dealing with stress, show them how scheduling or journaling helps you. If they see positive results, they might be open to learning more about your faith.
- **Stay Respectful**: Not everyone will accept your views, but you can keep showing grace and kindness. You never know when seeds planted today might grow later.

11. Avoiding Pride and Judgmental Attitudes

With a strong foundation, you may feel more secure than those still searching for stability. Make sure this does not turn into pride. Looking down on others for their struggles or choices is not godly.

- **Practice Empathy**: Instead of judging someone for a poor choice, consider what pressures they might be under. This does not mean you excuse wrongdoing, but you remain compassionate.
- **Offer Hope, Not Condemnation**: If someone seeks advice, focus on solutions and encouragement rather than blame.
- **Keep Learning**: Remind yourself that you are still a work in progress. A strong foundation does not mean perfect living; it means having the right base from which to learn and grow.

---

12. Using Technology to Strengthen Your Base

We live in a digital age, and smartphones or computers can either help or hurt your foundation depending on how you use them.

- **Bible Apps and Devotionals**: There are many applications that send daily Bible verses or allow you to set reading goals. Use them to stay consistent.
- **Christian Podcasts and Sermons**: Listening to good teachings on your way to school or during breaks can keep your mind on track.
- **Social Media Boundaries**: Be aware of the content you consume. If certain accounts lead you into comparison or negative thinking, do a quick clean-up of who you follow.

---

13. Handling Setbacks and Slumps

Even strong Christians can experience periods where they feel less motivated or slip into bad habits. This does not mean you have lost your foundation; it just means you need to refocus.

- **Admit the Problem Quickly**: The longer you pretend everything is fine, the harder it is to bounce back.

- **Seek Help**: Prayer is your first resort, but also reach out to someone you trust. A Christian friend or leader can give you advice.
- **Use Scripture**: Find verses that speak to your specific struggle. Read them aloud daily. The word of God is powerful in reshaping thoughts.

---

14. Strengthening Faith Through Trials

Difficult times can actually strengthen your foundation if you stay close to God.

- **Recognize God's Presence**: Remember that God never leaves you, even when life is hard. This knowledge can carry you through.
- **Look for Personal Growth**: Trials often reveal weak spots in your character. Instead of feeling defeated, focus on improving those areas.
- **Give Testimony**: Later on, when you have come through the trial, you can share how it helped you grow stronger in faith. This encourages others in their own hard times.

---

15. Making Room for God Each Day

A strong foundation is not built overnight. It is formed by small daily choices that eventually create a lasting structure in your life. Make room for God in your schedule, and you will see changes in how you think and act.

- **Start the Day with Prayer**: Even a short prayer in the morning can set the tone for the day.
- **Read a Portion of Scripture**: Choose a manageable amount. It could be just a few verses if you are short on time.
- **End the Day Reflecting**: At night, thank God for blessings and see if there is anything you need to correct or improve.

---

16. Checking Your Foundation Regularly

Just as a house needs regular inspection to stay strong, your spiritual life needs consistent checks:

- **Monitor Your Fruit**: Are you showing love, patience, kindness, and self-control in your daily life? If you see these qualities slipping, it may be time to reinforce your foundation with prayer and scripture reading.
- **Ask for Feedback**: Sometimes, it helps to hear from trusted friends or mentors. They might notice warning signs you miss.
- **Stay Open to Correction**: Do not get defensive when someone points out an area of growth. Use it as a chance to strengthen that part of your life.

---

17. Real-Life Examples of Strong Foundations

Many successful Christian teens credit their stability to a steady routine of prayer, reading the Bible, and regularly discussing their faith with mentors. Some wake up early to have quiet time with God. Others dedicate part of their lunch break to reading a devotional. These are not just random acts but deliberate habits that build a strong base.

A Unique Strategy: Some teens write "I rely on God" on the first page of their school notebook. Each time they open it, they see that reminder. This small act helps them keep God in mind throughout the day.

---

18. The Relationship Between Belief and Action

It is easy to say you believe in Christian values, but your real foundation is shown in how you act. A strong base leads to consistent good actions:

- **Integrity**: You do the right thing even when no one is watching.
- **Steadfastness**: You remain calm and hopeful in the face of obstacles.
- **Kindness**: Your respect for others stays the same whether they are popular or not.

Actions speak louder than words. When your foundation is strong, people can see it in how you treat them and how you handle life's challenges.

---

19. Overcoming Cultural Pressures

Teenage years often involve dealing with cultural norms that clash with Christian values. Media might push certain looks, behaviors, or moral stances that go against what you believe. A firm foundation helps you weigh cultural trends against biblical truths.

- **Critical Thinking**: Look at a trend or lifestyle critically. Does it uplift godly values or lead you away from them?
- **Be Willing to Stand Out**: Sometimes, following God means you will not blend in perfectly with the crowd. Be prepared for that.
- **Choose Long-Term Benefits Over Short-Term Approval**: Following the crowd might make you feel accepted for a moment, but it could harm your faith or future. A strong foundation pushes you to think beyond the immediate moment.

---

20. Moving Forward with Confidence

As you keep building and maintaining your foundation, you will find more peace. Life will still have ups and downs, but you will be anchored in faith. This solid base allows you to grow into the person God designed you to be.

Questions for Reflection

1. Which daily habit can you start to build or strengthen your foundation?
2. Do you have moral guidelines in place to guide your choices?
3. How can you stay connected with a Christian community for support?

Practical Action Point
Pick one habit (like morning prayer or evening Bible reading) and commit to it for two weeks straight. Track your progress in a journal or on your phone's calendar. After two weeks, assess how this habit has affected your day-to-day life and your sense of closeness to God.

Conclusion to Chapter 2
Building a strong foundation is about more than just avoiding mistakes. It is a deliberate process of nurturing faith, discipline, and healthy habits. Through regular Bible study, prayer, moral boundaries, and wise decision-making, you set the stage for a successful and meaningful life. In the chapters ahead, you will discover more specific ways to apply these principles to real-life issues, such as dealing with stress, forming strong friendships, and staying pure in heart and mind.

CHAPTER 3

Managing Stress and Worry

Introduction
Life as a teen can feel overwhelming. You have school tests, friend dramas, family expectations, and a list of things you have to do every day. On top of that, you see social media posts that can add even more pressure. It is no surprise that many teenage girls experience stress and worry. However, stress does not have to control your life. You can learn simple but powerful methods to handle it in a way that lines up with Christian teachings.

In this chapter, we will talk about practical techniques for dealing with stress and worry. We will also look at spiritual truths that can help you stay calm when problems come up. By combining practical steps and faith-based wisdom, you can find peace in your heart, even in uncertain times.

---

1. Recognizing the Signs of Stress and Worry

Stress is not always obvious. Sometimes it appears in ways you might not notice at first. You could feel more tired than usual, get headaches, or find yourself snapping at friends and family. You might even feel guilty for no clear reason. Recognizing these signs is the first step in handling stress properly.

- **Physical Clues**: Headaches, stomachaches, and muscle tension can be signals of stress. Notice if these happen often, especially during busy school weeks or conflict with friends.
- **Emotional Clues**: Feeling irritable, sad, or anxious might point to worry building up inside. Pay attention to mood swings or feelings of panic.
- **Behavioral Changes**: Some people avoid their responsibilities or overeat. Others can't sleep well at night. Any sudden or repeated changes in behavior could indicate rising stress levels.

A Useful Approach: Keep a small journal. Write down how you feel each day, physically and emotionally. Note any big or small events that happened. This record helps you see patterns. If you notice that every time you have a math quiz you get a headache, you can plan how to handle that stress before it becomes overwhelming.

2. Common Causes of Stress for Christian Teen Girls

While some stress factors are universal, others might be more unique to Christian teens. For instance, feeling pressure to live out your faith can add extra layers of worry. Here are some common triggers:

1. **Academic Load**: Tests, homework, and grades can put a heavy load on your mind.
2. **Family Expectations**: You might worry about pleasing parents who want you to do well.
3. **Church Involvement**: You may feel pressure to volunteer, attend services, or meet spiritual expectations.
4. **Social Media Comparisons**: Seeing peers who seem perfect online can make you feel like you are not measuring up.
5. **Moral Conflicts**: You might be torn between living by Christian values and fitting in with popular trends.

Deep Insight: Sometimes, you might not even realize that a conflict between your faith and worldly influences is causing stress. For example, if your friends are pressuring you to watch certain shows that go against your moral standards, you might feel uneasy without fully understanding why. Recognizing the conflict is the first step to resolving the stress it brings.

---

3. Grounding Yourself in God's Peace

The Bible talks about giving our worries to God. One verse (Philippians 4:6-7) reminds us not to be anxious but to pray about everything. This is a direct invitation from God to turn our stress into a time of prayer. But how can you do this practically?

- **Setting Aside Worry Time**: This might sound strange, but choose a short block of time each day (maybe 10 minutes) to lay your worries before God. List them out if you need to. Pray or think quietly about them, asking for wisdom. When the time is up, move forward with the day. This practice can help you avoid letting worry take over your whole day.

- **Using Breathing and Scripture**: When stress hits, close your eyes, take a deep breath, and slowly exhale. As you do, recall a comforting verse like, "God is my refuge and strength" (Psalm 46:1). Repeat it in your mind a few times. This simple method links body and spirit, reducing physical tension and reminding you that God is with you.
- **Continuing Communication with God**: Instead of only praying in the morning or at night, say short prayers throughout the day. For instance, right before a class test, simply say, "God, please help me focus and give me peace." Keeping God in the loop helps anchor you when stress tries to take over.

---

4. Setting Realistic Goals and Expectations

Some stress is self-made, arising from impossible goals. You might want perfect grades, a lead role in a school play, and a busy social life all at once. While being ambitious is fine, stretching yourself too thin can lead to burnout.

- **Prioritizing Tasks**: Write down what you need to do for the week. Rank them by importance. Focus on the top tasks first. If you have extra time and energy, work on the others.
- **Allowing Room for Rest**: The Bible mentions rest, such as the Sabbath principle, reminding us that rest is a part of a balanced life. Dedicate at least one afternoon a week to recharging. This might be reading a favorite book, taking a walk, or just sitting quietly.
- **Letting Go of Perfection**: Accept that you are human. You will make mistakes. Seek excellence but not flawlessness. This change in perspective can reduce a lot of pressure.

Rare Idea: Sometimes, you can schedule a "no-activity window." Pick a small part of the day where you have zero commitments—no phone, no chores, no homework. Use this time to reflect on God's presence or simply unwind. This short break can work like a mental reset.

5. Healthy Ways to Release Tension

When stress mounts, your mind and body need safe outlets to let go of the tension. Activities like exercise, listening to calming music, or even creative hobbies can help.

1. **Physical Activities**: Sports, dancing in your room, or just going for a short run can lower stress hormones and help clear your mind.
2. **Creative Outlets**: Drawing, writing, playing an instrument, or crafting can give your mind a break from worries. It is a constructive way to process feelings.
3. **Talking It Out**: Find a trusted adult, sibling, or friend who can listen. Often, just speaking your worries out loud helps you see them in a more manageable way.

Advanced Tip: Some Christian teens use creative projects to reflect their faith. For example, you might write a short poem expressing your trust in God. This not only relieves stress but also strengthens your connection to His truths.

---

6. Identifying Faulty Thinking

Stress often grows when we feed ourselves untrue or exaggerated thoughts. For example, if you believe "I'll fail at everything if I don't get top grades," you are placing too much weight on a single outcome. Recognizing these thoughts can stop worry from growing.

- **Common Negative Thoughts**: "I'm worthless if I don't succeed." "Nobody cares about me." "I have to do everything perfectly."
- **Replacing Them with Truths**: Counter each negative idea with a fact. For instance, "My value isn't based on grades" or "There are people who love me and look out for me."
- **Biblical Support**: Look for verses that speak against these false beliefs. You can even keep a small note with a list of these truths to remind yourself daily.

7. Trusting God's Control

One reason we worry is the feeling we have to solve every problem alone. But the Bible tells us God is in control and loves His children. You might feel small or powerless in the face of big issues, yet remember you are not carrying these burdens alone.

- **Recognizing Limitations**: It is okay to admit you cannot handle everything. That is why prayer is so powerful—it points us to the One who can.
- **Learning to Surrender**: Surrendering does not mean giving up on goals or ignoring responsibilities. It means acknowledging that God oversees the bigger picture.
- **Gratitude**: When you notice stress rising, pause and thank God for simple things—clean water, a place to sleep, a friend who makes you laugh. This shifts your focus from fear to thankfulness.

Seldom Discussed Point: Spiritual surrender also involves handing over your timeline. You might want solutions right away, but God might work in a different way or at a different pace. Accepting this can ease the tension of unmet expectations.

---

8. Dealing with Stress in Friendships

Sometimes, stress comes from conflicts or misunderstandings with friends. You may worry about losing friends or being left out. This is common, but there are steps to address it:

1. **Open Communication**: If a friend has upset you, talk about it calmly instead of letting the stress build. Use "I statements," like, "I felt overlooked when…"
2. **Seeking Reconciliation**: If you share Christian values with your friend, remember that God wants unity among believers. Apologize when you are wrong, and offer forgiveness to others.
3. **Setting Boundaries**: If a friendship repeatedly causes stress and negative emotions, consider spending less time with that person. Sometimes, caring for your mental well-being means limiting contact with those who do not encourage you.

9. Practical Stress-Reduction Tools

Here are some lesser-known but effective methods you might find helpful:

- **Body Scan**: Lie down or sit in a chair. Close your eyes and focus on one body part at a time, from your toes up to your head. Breathe slowly as you move your attention. This relaxes your muscles and mind.
- **Music or Audio Bible**: Listening to peaceful music or an audio version of the Bible can set a calming atmosphere. Make a playlist of soothing songs or short passages.
- **Single-Task Focus**: In our multi-tasking world, switching between tasks quickly can cause stress. Try focusing on one thing at a time. For instance, when doing homework, silence your phone so you can give your full attention to the work.

10. Knowing When to Seek Help

Some stress is short-lived. Other times, it can feel overwhelming and persistent. If you notice your stress lasting for weeks or causing harmful behaviors (like constant crying, harming yourself, or extreme anxiety), it is time to seek help from an adult you trust, such as:

- **Parents or Guardians**: They might help by adjusting your home responsibilities or giving advice.
- **School Counselor**: Counselors are trained to help students deal with stress, and they can suggest coping methods that suit your situation.
- **Pastor or Youth Leader**: Someone with strong spiritual grounding can pray with you and guide you to see biblical truths that bring peace.
- **Medical Professional**: In cases where stress affects your daily life severely, a doctor or therapist might be needed.

Rarely Discussed Fact: Some Christians think that feeling anxious is a sign of weak faith, so they hesitate to talk to professionals. In reality, seeking help is not a sign of lack of faith. It can be a wise step toward healing and better mental health, which pleases God as we care for the bodies and minds He gave us.

11. Handling Stress at School

School is a major stress point for many teens, especially if you juggle multiple classes, extracurriculars, and social pressures. Here are specific tips:

1. **Organize Your Space**: Keep your notes and textbooks tidy. A cluttered workspace can increase stress.
2. **Plan Your Study Times**: Break projects into smaller tasks and schedule them on a calendar so you don't rush at the last minute.
3. **Use Study Groups Wisely**: Studying with friends can help if you actually focus on the material. If the group becomes a social hangout, it might add more stress later when you realize you still have not prepared enough.
4. **Ask Teachers for Guidance**: If a concept is difficult, asking a teacher or tutor is better than stressing alone. Many teachers appreciate students who show they care about understanding the material.

12. Minimizing Worry About the Future

Teens often worry about future plans: college, career, or how life will turn out. While it is good to plan, overthinking future details can lead to stress today.

- **Focus on Present Faithfulness**: Take care of what you can do today—study well, help at home, grow your skills. Trust that if you do your best now, God will guide you to the right future.
- **Explore Options**: If college is on your mind, research schools or programs that interest you. Having knowledge reduces uncertainty.
- **Seek Wise Counsel**: Talk with mentors, teachers, or older friends who have been through this stage. They can help you see realistic steps for the future.

Unique Thought: Sometimes, writing a "5-year prayer list" can calm your worries. You list out hopes and concerns for the future, then pray over them once a week. This way, you hand your future to God but still acknowledge the steps you need to take.

13. Spiritual Practices for Stress Relief

Since you are a Christian, do not underestimate the power of spiritual habits:

- **Praise and Worship**: Singing or listening to worship songs can shift your focus from the problem to the One who can solve it.
- **Reading Psalms**: Many psalms deal with fear and stress. Seeing how the writers expressed their worries and then trusted God can calm your own heart.
- **Scripture Meditation**: Pick a short verse, repeat it, and reflect on it. This helps fill your mind with God's truth rather than your own anxious thoughts.

---

14. Dealing with Stress in Sports and Activities

Being on a sports team or in a club can be fun, but it can also bring stress, especially if you feel pressured to excel or meet external expectations.

- **Balance Your Schedule**: If you notice you have too many activities, consider dropping one. Quality is often better than quantity.
- **Remember Your Motive**: If you joined an activity because you love it, keep that in mind. Don't let the fun get buried under pressure to outperform everyone else.
- **Share Stress with Teammates**: If your stress is related to team conflicts or performance anxiety, talk to teammates or a coach. Working together can lighten the load.

---

15. Creating a Support Network

You don't have to face stress on your own. Actively build a network of supportive people:

- **Trusted Friends**: Friends who encourage you, remind you of God's truths, and respect your values are priceless.

- **Adults Who Care**: This could be a parent, aunt, older cousin, or church leader. Having someone more experienced to guide you makes a huge difference.
- **Faith-Based Groups**: Joining a youth group or Bible study can connect you with other believers who face similar challenges.

Seldom Mentioned Advice: Ask your support network to pray specifically for your stress points. Sharing specific prayer requests (like an upcoming big test or family conflict) allows them to pray with clarity.

16. The Importance of Good Self-Talk

What you say to yourself affects how you handle stress. If you constantly scold yourself, you add tension to an already stressful situation. Instead, learn positive self-talk grounded in biblical truth.

- **Address Mistakes in a Constructive Way**: Instead of thinking "I'm hopeless," say "I made a mistake here, but I can learn from it."
- **Encourage Yourself with Scripture**: Remind yourself, "I can do all things through Christ who gives me strength" (Philippians 4:13).
- **Stay Realistic**: Don't make everything seem perfect in your head. Acknowledge challenges, but believe that, with God's help, you can face them.

17. Dealing with Stress from Social Media

Social media is a big part of many teens' lives, but it can raise stress levels if used incorrectly. You might compare yourself to others or see upsetting posts.

- **Set Time Limits**: Decide how much time you will allow yourself on social media each day. Turn off notifications to avoid constant distractions.
- **Curate Your Feed**: Unfollow or mute accounts that bring you down or encourage harmful thoughts. Follow accounts that post wholesome or inspiring content.
- **Take Breaks**: Consider a social media "fast" for a day or a weekend. Use that time to do something nurturing for your mind or spirit.

18. Growing from Stressful Moments

Stressful situations can actually teach you valuable lessons if you view them from a growth mindset. For instance:

- **Developing Empathy**: Going through your own stresses can help you understand others who struggle.
- **Practicing Problem-Solving**: When you face a challenge, you learn ways to fix or handle it better next time.
- **Strengthening Faith**: Seeing God come through in tough situations deepens your trust in Him for future problems.

Rare Insight: Some people keep a "stress victory list." Whenever you overcome a stressful event—like passing a difficult test or resolving a conflict—you note it down. Later, when new worries come, you look back and remember how you succeeded before, which boosts your confidence in God's guidance.

19. Encouraging Others Who Are Stressed

When you notice a friend or sibling dealing with stress, you can offer help:

1. **Listen Without Judgment**: Simply hearing someone out can ease their burden.
2. **Pray with Them**: If they are open to prayer, offering a quick prayer for peace can be comforting.
3. **Suggest Resources**: Share verses or methods that have helped you. Recommend a book or a sermon online that speaks to stress or worry.

Helping others not only lifts them up, but it can also lessen your own stress. Acting kindly towards someone who is stressed can give you a sense of purpose and reduce focus on your own anxieties.

20. Moving Forward with Less Worry

Stress and worry do not have to rule your life. By identifying the causes, relying on God, and using practical tools, you can keep stress at a healthy level. This does not mean life will always be easy, but it does mean you can stay calm and centered no matter what happens.

Questions for Reflection

1. What is one thing that causes you the most stress? How can you address it differently today?
2. Which methods from this chapter do you want to try first?
3. How can you include others in your plan to lower stress—through prayer or simple acts of kindness?

Practical Action Point
Pick one stress management approach and practice it consistently for at least one week. This might be journaling, daily prayer breaks, or a regular walk outside. Keep track of any changes in how you feel. By focusing on just one positive habit, you are more likely to stick with it and see real progress.

Conclusion to Chapter 3
Handling stress and worry is about recognizing its sources, trusting God, and applying practical steps to find relief. Whether you face pressure from school, friends, or personal expectations, these methods help you stay stable. You do not have to let stress weigh you down. Instead, you can learn to lean on God's strength while also making wise choices that protect your mental and emotional health.

CHAPTER 4

Making Healthy Friendships

Introduction
Friendships shape our teenage years in big ways. The bonds you form can give you joy, support, and memories that last a lifetime. However, picking the right friends and being a good friend yourself is not always straightforward. Sometimes, you might feel pressure to fit in, leading you toward connections that are not helpful. Other times, you might feel alone, unsure how to find friends who share your faith and values.

This chapter will explain how to build strong friendships that add goodness to your life. You will learn tips to identify friends who push you to grow in positive ways, and you will discover ways to handle problems that come up in friendships. Since this is a self-help book for Christian teen girls, we will also talk about how faith influences friendships.

---

1. The Purpose of Friendship

In the Bible, friends are seen as people who can love, support, and sharpen one another. Proverbs 27:17 says, "As iron sharpens iron, so one person sharpens another." True friendship goes beyond just hanging out together. It involves understanding, support, honesty, and helping each other grow.

- **Emotional Support**: A real friend offers a listening ear when you are upset and shares in your excitement when things go well.
- **Spiritual Encouragement**: In a Christian context, friends can pray together, study God's Word, and keep each other responsible in faith.
- **Growth Partner**: True friends help you learn from mistakes, improve your character, and inspire you to reach your goals.

Rare Note: While it is fun to have many acquaintances, a few close friendships often provide deeper connection. Quality is more important than quantity.

---

2. Finding the Right People

Sometimes, you might think finding good friends is a matter of luck, but you can take steps to meet people who have positive traits and values:

1. **Get Involved**: Join church activities, youth groups, or school clubs where people have similar interests. Being in these environments makes it easier to get to know new people.
2. **Look for Character, Not Popularity**: Focus on people who show kindness and honesty, not just those who are in the "in" crowd.
3. **Pay Attention to How They Treat Others**: Notice if a potential friend acts differently around different groups or shows respect to everyone. This can hint at how they might treat you in the long run.

Practical Thought: If you can volunteer for a community project or a church outreach, you might meet people who care about serving others. Shared experiences of helping can create strong bonds from the start.

---

3. Becoming a Good Friend First

Friendship is a two-way street. If you want supportive friends, you must be supportive as well.

- **Listen Actively**: When a friend shares something personal, give them your full attention without interruption.
- **Offer Help**: Small acts like helping with homework, giving someone a ride, or providing a shoulder to cry on can deepen trust.
- **Keep Your Word**: If you promise to do something, follow through. Reliability is the backbone of any solid relationship.

Seldom Mentioned Tip: Even small gestures like remembering a friend's birthday or sending a text when they are sad can make a big difference in strengthening your bond.

4. Understanding Different Levels of Friendship

Not all friendships are the same. Some people are casual friends you say hello to at school, while others are close friends you share deep secrets with. Recognizing these levels can help you set the right expectations:

- **Acquaintances**: You see them around, know a bit about them, but rarely share personal details.
- **Casual Friends**: You hang out more often, but the relationship is still light.
- **Close Friends**: You feel comfortable being vulnerable. You share highs and lows, and you trust each other.
- **Mentors**: They may be older or more experienced. They guide and advise you, but it is still a form of friendship.

Deep Insight: Mixing up these levels can cause hurt feelings. You might expect a casual friend to act like a close friend, but they are not ready to share that level of trust. Being aware of the differences can save you from misunderstandings.

---

5. Balancing Christian Values with Friendship Choices

Not all your friends need to be Christians, but it's wise to have at least a few who share your faith. They can strengthen your spiritual walk and offer godly advice. With friends who are not Christians, it is important to remain respectful and kind while also staying true to your values.

- **Healthy Influence**: Choose friends who build you up, not those who pull you away from a good lifestyle or beliefs.
- **Avoid Being Unequally Tied Down**: If a friend repeatedly pushes you to ignore your faith, you might want to limit how much personal information and time you share with them.
- **Showing Love to All**: Jesus spent time with a variety of people. You can still be friendly with classmates of different beliefs without compromising your own.

Warning: If a group of friends always draws you into harmful habits, it might be time to step back. You should not sacrifice your well-being or faith to keep those friendships.

6. Handling Friendship Conflicts

Arguments and misunderstandings can happen, even in the best friendships. Knowing how to handle them in a godly way can save the relationship or at least end conflicts peacefully.

- **Calm Communication**: Speak directly and kindly about the issue. Avoid gossip or harsh language.
- **Listening to Their Side**: They might have reasons you did not consider. Hearing them out can make a big difference.
- **Asking for Forgiveness**: If you realize you were wrong, apologize sincerely. Don't let pride stop you from making things right.
- **Seeking Mediation**: If the problem is big and you can't solve it alone, ask a trusted adult or mentor to help you both talk it through.

Little-Known Advice: Sometimes, time apart can help both parties cool down and think clearly. It is okay to take a short break before trying to mend the friendship, as long as you plan to resolve the matter soon.

7. Establishing Healthy Boundaries

Friendship does not mean you have to share every single thought or be together 24/7. Boundaries protect your emotional and mental health.

- **Time Boundaries**: Set limits on how often you hang out, especially if you need to study, have family time, or simply recharge.
- **Emotional Boundaries**: You can share personal details at a pace you are comfortable with. If you feel uneasy about discussing a topic, it is okay to say so.
- **Physical Boundaries**: Even in friendships, you have the right to personal space. A hug might be fine, but you might feel uneasy about other forms of closeness, and that is valid.

Unique Thought: Some teens mistake boundary-setting for being unfriendly. In truth, setting healthy limits can protect the friendship from unhealthy dynamics and misunderstandings.

8. When Friends Make Different Choices

Sometimes, friends you cherish might choose to act in ways you do not agree with, such as experimenting with harmful behaviors. You might wonder whether to keep being their friend or to distance yourself.

- **Show Concern**: Let them know you care about them and are worried. Offer help if they want to make a change.
- **Stay True to Your Standards**: Do not feel pressured to join in the behavior just to maintain the friendship.
- **Know When to Step Back**: If their choices repeatedly harm you or they ridicule your beliefs, it is okay to reduce contact for your well-being.

Crucial Note: Always pray for friends who have gone off track. God can work in their lives. You do not have to carry the entire burden alone, but your prayers can make a difference.

---

9. Building Trust in Friendships

Trust is earned over time. Small acts of honesty and loyalty form a strong bond.

- **Keep Secrets Private**: If a friend confides in you, do not share it with others without permission.
- **Be Consistent**: If one day you are supportive and the next you ignore them, trust breaks down. Show stable behavior as much as possible.
- **Give Them the Benefit of the Doubt**: If you hear a rumor about a friend, ask them directly before you assume it is true.

Underrated Tip: Even in a trusting friendship, you should still use discernment. Do not put yourself in a position where your secrets can be used against you. Slow and steady trust-building is usually safer than revealing everything at once.

---

10. Friendship Across Different Ages

You can learn from people younger or older than you. Younger friends might bring a fresh viewpoint, while older friends or mentors can share life lessons.

- **Older Mentors**: They can guide you in matters of faith or practical life skills.
- **Younger Friends**: Helping them can strengthen your leadership and empathy.
- **Same-Age Friends**: Shared experiences help you feel understood and supported.

Lesser-Known Benefit: Friendships across age groups can break down stereotypes. They also widen your understanding of the world, which can help you develop a more caring heart.

---

11. Navigating Technology and Friendship

Social media and messaging apps let friends connect in new ways, but also bring challenges.

- **Online Etiquette**: Avoid posting things that could hurt your friends, like private details or mean comments.
- **Managing Group Chats**: Big group chats can spark drama. If arguments start, consider suggesting a calm talk in person.
- **Avoid Oversharing**: The internet never forgets. If you would not say something face to face, do not say it online.

Advanced Thought: Video calls or voice messages can sometimes be more personal than typed messages. Hearing each other's tone of voice can reduce misunderstandings that often happen through text alone.

---

12. Friendship and Peer Pressure

Even a good friend can pressure you to do something you are not okay with, such as skipping class or being unkind to someone. Standing firm requires courage.

- **Stay Prepared**: Think ahead about what you will say if a friend pressures you. Practice a polite refusal like, "I'm not comfortable with that."

- **Suggest Alternatives**: If your friend wants to do something that feels wrong, offer a different idea: "Instead of that, why don't we...?"
- **Stick to Your Beliefs**: If they ignore your boundaries or keep pushing, you might have to limit how much time you spend with them.

Important Reminder: True friends respect your convictions. If you always have to fight against their influence, it may be time to question if that friendship is healthy.

---

13. Taking Friendship Slow

Some friendships form quickly, while others grow slowly over time. Both can be valid, but it's often safer to take time to really know someone's character.

- **Early Caution**: People can put on a pleasant face at first. Notice how they act in various settings, such as under stress or when others are not around.
- **Allow Deep Bonding Slowly**: Share lighter personal details before revealing deeper ones. Let trust build naturally.
- **Avoid Desperation**: If you are lonely, you might want to latch on to any friend you can find. But it's better to wait for a relationship that is genuinely wholesome than to jump into one that causes harm.

---

14. Serving Together

One of the fastest ways to strengthen friendships is to serve together—whether it is volunteering at a local food bank, helping out at church events, or supporting a neighborhood cleanup.

- **Shared Purpose**: Working side by side creates unity and fosters deeper conversation.
- **Teamwork**: Seeing how you and your friend handle teamwork reveals a lot about how supportive and reliable you both are.
- **Memory Building**: Serving creates shared experiences that become positive memories in the future.

Hidden Bonus: Serving others often reduces stress and self-focus. It also reminds you both of the bigger picture—loving and helping those around you, which strengthens your bond.

15. Positive Communication Skills

Healthy friendships rely on clear, kind communication. This does not mean you have to agree on everything, but it does mean talking in a respectful way.

- **Speak Truth Lovingly**: If you must correct a friend, do it gently, focusing on actions rather than attacking their character.
- **Use "I" Statements**: "I feel hurt when you cancel plans last minute," instead of "You always do this."
- **Show Genuine Interest**: Ask questions about their day, family, or hobbies. Listen and respond thoughtfully.

Practical Idea: Sometimes, clarifying what you heard them say can prevent misunderstandings. After they speak, reply with something like, "So you are saying you felt embarrassed at practice?" This gives them a chance to correct any misunderstandings.

16. Getting Through Friendship Disappointments

Friends might let you down sometimes. They could forget important dates, break a promise, or be too busy. While this can hurt, it is also part of being human.

- **Manage Expectations**: Everyone has flaws. Your friend might have areas of weakness just like you do.
- **Offer Forgiveness**: We all need grace at times. If the friend is genuinely sorry, giving them another chance can lead to even stronger trust.
- **Learn to Let Go**: If disappointments happen constantly and the friendship is one-sided, it might be time to accept that you have grown apart.

Deeper Lesson: Handling disappointments with grace is a reflection of how God extends grace to us. Even if the friendship ends, acting lovingly can give closure and peace.

17. Long-Distance Friendships

Sometimes, a best friend might move to another city or you might switch schools. Maintaining friendships from a distance is possible with effort.

- **Regular Check-Ins**: Schedule a weekly video call or send messages to catch up on each other's lives.
- **Share Moments**: You can swap pictures or voice clips of daily happenings. This helps you feel involved in each other's life.
- **Plan Occasional Visits**: If possible, arrange to visit each other during holidays. If not, plan special online get-togethers.

Lesser-Known Tip: Distance can sometimes deepen friendships because both parties must communicate intentionally and appreciate each other's time more.

---

18. Encouraging Each Other's Faith

If you have friends who share your Christian beliefs, you can support one another in spiritual growth:

- **Pray Together**: Even a brief prayer before a big test or problem can unite you.
- **Bible Study**: Consider reading the same Bible passage and discussing it. This can be done in person or through a group chat.
- **Accountability**: If you are trying to stick to certain good habits, ask a friend to check in on you weekly to see how you are doing.

Rare Suggestion: Some friends make a "prayer jar" where they each write down prayer requests. Over time, they open the jar to see which requests were answered. This not only nurtures faith but also bonds the friendship.

---

19. Dealing with Jealousy in Friendships

Jealousy can creep in if a friend achieves something you wanted or becomes closer to another friend. This feeling can strain the relationship if not handled well.

- **Acknowledge Your Feelings**: It is normal to feel a bit envious sometimes. Admitting it is the first step to resolving it.
- **Work on Self-Confidence**: Remind yourself of your own gifts and how God made you unique.
- **Celebrate Their Wins**: Instead of letting jealousy turn you bitter, choose to be happy for your friend's success. A true friend learns to be glad for the other person's blessings.

Healthy Approach: If jealousy persists, talk to a wise adult or mentor. They can offer tips on how to shift your perspective. Sometimes, underlying insecurities cause jealousy, and working through those can improve your overall self-esteem.

---

20. Looking Ahead

Friendships can change over time. People grow, move, or switch interests. It is okay to let some friendships evolve. The key is to remain respectful, honest, and kind as seasons shift.

Questions for Reflection

1. How do you decide if someone would be a good friend for you?
2. What kind of friend do you want to be for others?
3. Are there any friendships in your life that need healthier boundaries or possibly a graceful ending?

Practical Action Point
This week, pick one friend you appreciate and do something kind for them. It could be a heartfelt note, a small gift that shows you listen to their interests, or simply an offer to help them study. Notice how a small, thoughtful action can deepen your bond.

Conclusion to Chapter 4
Friendships are a precious part of life, especially during the teenage years. By choosing friends wisely, being a trustworthy friend yourself, and keeping Christ in your interactions, you can form connections that bring lasting encouragement and joy. When conflicts arise, handle them with respect and clear communication. Understand that it is fine to have friends of different backgrounds, but keep your values intact.

CHAPTER 5

Handling Social Media and Technology

Introduction

Technology is a big part of daily life for most teenagers. It connects you with friends and keeps you entertained. It can also be a place to learn new things. However, spending too much time online or following the wrong kind of content can lead to negative feelings, comparison, or even harm your walk of faith.

In this chapter, we will look at ways to use social media and technology in a healthy manner that honors God and supports your well-being. You will find practical ideas, deeper insights, and tips to avoid the pitfalls that many teens face. Rather than simply saying "use less phone," this section will explain how to make positive decisions that can keep you balanced and rooted in Christian values.

---

1. Understanding Technology's Role in Your Life

Technology itself is not evil or good; it is a tool. You decide how to use it. The internet can be a channel for godly inspiration if you follow encouraging accounts and learn new skills. On the other hand, it can be destructive if it pushes you toward harmful behaviors or constant comparison.

- **Balance**: Do you feel glued to your phone? Do you ignore real-life interactions to check notifications? Keeping an eye on how much you use devices is the first step to managing them well.
- **Purpose**: Think about why you use social media. Is it to stay in touch with friends, learn new hobbies, or just scroll mindlessly? Clarifying your purpose helps you avoid wasting time and energy.

Rarely Discussed Insight: Some people set "tech boundaries" not just for how long they are online, but also for what times of day they use technology. For instance, they might avoid screen time in the early morning to start the day with prayer or Bible reading. This can greatly improve mental clarity and spiritual focus.

2. Setting Wise Boundaries Online

If you let social media run your life, it can become a source of stress and temptation. Setting boundaries keeps it in check, so you have a healthier relationship with technology.

1. **Time Limits**: You can install apps that track your screen time and gently remind you when you have hit your daily limit. This ensures you do not spend hours scrolling without realizing it.
2. **Content Filters**: If certain types of content lead you away from good habits or make you anxious, use built-in filters or block specific sites.
3. **Tech-Free Zones**: Some families decide that meal times, bedrooms, or study sessions are off-limits for phones. This reduces distractions and encourages real connection.

Practical Example: Try keeping your phone out of your bedroom at night. Many teens sleep better when they do not have the constant buzz of notifications. Good rest is essential for your health and your focus during the day.

---

3. Avoiding Comparison and Envy

One of the biggest problems with social media is the temptation to compare your life with others. You see a friend's perfect photo or read about someone's achievements and start feeling bad about yourself.

- **Remember It's a Highlight Reel**: People usually post their best moments. You rarely see their struggles or normal days. So you are comparing your behind-the-scenes to their bright moments.
- **Count Your Blessings**: Focus on what God has already given you—talents, people in your life, opportunities—and thank Him for them. This mind shift helps you avoid envy.
- **Mute or Unfollow**: If certain accounts consistently make you feel inadequate or push negative content, it is okay to mute or unfollow them. It is not about being mean; it is about protecting your heart.

Deeper Thought: Social media often shows physical looks, clothes, or fun experiences. However, a person's worth is much more than that. True identity lies in being a child of God, not in appearing flawless on a screen.

4. Online Friendships vs. Real-Life Connections

Technology allows you to meet people from around the world, but online friendships can be tricky.

- **Safety First**: Never share personal details like your address or phone number with strangers. Use wisdom and talk to a trusted adult if you are unsure.
- **Know the Difference**: While online friendships can be meaningful, they are often missing key elements of real-life interaction (like face-to-face conversations and shared experiences).
- **Quality Over Quantity**: Having countless online "friends" or "followers" does not guarantee genuine support. Real relationships—online or offline—are built on trust, respect, and honesty.

Rare Tip: Some teens schedule "virtual hangouts" with close friends who live far away. They share a screen, watch a show together, or do a Bible study through video chat. This can deepen an online connection and keep it from feeling shallow.

5. Using Technology for Growth and Service

Rather than seeing phones and computers as distractions, view them as tools to help you grow and help others.

- **Online Devotionals and Bible Studies**: Many websites and apps offer daily readings, video lessons, or group studies. Joining one can keep you in the Word and allow you to discuss Scripture with friends.
- **Serving Others Online**: You could post encouraging verses or stories on social media, offer homework help to classmates, or organize charitable fundraisers. Technology can expand your reach for good.
- **Learning New Skills**: You can find tutorials on cooking, art, coding, music, and more. Using technology to develop a skill can enrich your life and boost your confidence.

Hidden Advantage: Sometimes, teens who feel shy in person are more comfortable reaching out online. This can open doors to helping and sharing your faith with people you would not normally talk to.

---

6. Handling Cyberbullying and Negative Comments

Sadly, the internet can be a place of bullying or harsh criticism. If you face cyberbullying, you do not have to suffer silently.

- **Document and Block**: Keep evidence of any harmful messages. Block or report the account. Most social media platforms have ways to address abusive behavior.
- **Talk to an Adult**: If the harassment continues or makes you feel unsafe, tell a parent, teacher, or counselor. You do not have to handle it alone.
- **Respond Wisely**: While it may be tempting to get into an online war of words, it is often best to stay calm, not reply to insults, and step away from the confrontation.

Faith-Based Perspective: The Bible teaches us to treat others with kindness, even when they are unkind to us. This does not mean you allow abuse. It means you refuse to sink to a hateful level. Instead, you can protect yourself, seek help, and pray for the person being hurtful.

---

7. Modesty and Integrity in the Digital World

Your online presence should match your offline values. Consider how modesty and integrity apply to social media posts and browsing habits.

- **Modesty in Photos and Language**: If you would be uncomfortable wearing or saying something at church, then it is probably wise not to post it online. Consistency is key.
- **Avoid Gossip**: It is easy to share rumors or negative talk online. Instead, choose words that build up others.
- **Stay True in Private**: Even in direct messages or private chats, keep your speech honest and respectful. God sees everything we do, online or not.

Deeper Reflection: Ask yourself, "Would I be okay if my parents, pastor, or future employer saw what I post?" Remember that digital footprints last a long time.

---

8. Spiritual Discernment in Media Choices

Beyond social media, there are movies, TV shows, music, and games at your fingertips. Not all content is beneficial, and some can slowly affect your thoughts or values.

- **Rate Your Content**: If a show or song uses language or shows images that clash with your beliefs, consider skipping it. Constant exposure to negativity can slowly dull your sense of right and wrong.
- **Read Reviews**: Before watching or playing something new, check reviews from trusted Christian sources or from people who have similar values.
- **Honor the Holy Spirit**: If you feel uneasy about something, pay attention to that feeling. Often, it is God's way of guiding you away from content that could harm you spiritually.

Rare Strategy: Some teens keep a personal "media log" for a week, noting what they watch or listen to. Then they check how each piece of content made them feel or act. This helps identify patterns and cut back on things that have a negative effect.

---

9. Creating Healthy Routines

If you allow it, technology can consume hours of your life each day. Creating routines can help you stay balanced.

- **Morning Routine**: Instead of checking your phone first, spend a few minutes in prayer or read a short Bible passage to set a positive tone.
- **Study Time**: During homework or revision, put your phone on silent or keep it in another room to avoid distractions.
- **Night Routine**: Decide a time when you will turn off screens—maybe 30 minutes before bed. Use that time to reflect on your day or do a calming activity.

Advanced Tip: If you really struggle to stick to a routine, involve a friend or family member. Tell them your plan and ask them to help you stay accountable. Sometimes, just knowing someone will ask, "Have you turned off your phone yet?" can help you follow through.

---

10. Balancing Online and Face-to-Face Interaction

One danger of technology is allowing it to replace real-life relationships. While online connections are useful, face-to-face communication builds deeper understanding and empathy.

- **Plan In-Person Meetups**: If it's safe and possible, schedule a coffee catch-up or a trip to the park with friends instead of always messaging.
- **Look Up**: Try putting your phone away when you are walking around or waiting in line. This might open unexpected chances to chat with someone near you.
- **Be Present**: When with family or friends in person, try to avoid constantly checking your phone. Show you value their company.

Lesser-Known Thought: Researchers have found that even having a phone on the table can reduce the quality of conversation because people expect interruptions. Keeping phones out of sight can lead to better bonding.

---

11. Recognizing Signs of Tech Addiction

It is possible to become so hooked on screens that you feel anxious when you are away from them. Some signals include:

- **Losing Track of Time**: You plan to watch one video, but suddenly an hour or two has passed.
- **Neglecting Responsibilities**: Homework, chores, or even personal hygiene slip because of screen time.
- **Feeling Irritable Without Your Device**: You get restless or upset when you cannot go online.
- **Worsening Mood After Use**: You feel more depressed or anxious after extended time on social media.

If these signs are familiar, consider speaking to a parent, mentor, or counselor. They can help you break free from unhealthy patterns.

12. Protecting Your Heart from Harmful Influences

The internet contains many things that go against Christian morals—violent images, explicit content, or people encouraging ungodly behavior. It is important to take steps to guard your heart.

- **Accountability Software**: Some families use software that reports your online activity to a parent or accountability partner. This can help you resist temptations.
- **Avoid Late-Night Browsing**: Many teens feel more tempted to check inappropriate sites when alone at night. Setting a tech curfew can protect you.
- **Stay Open About Struggles**: If you slip into harmful viewing habits, do not hide it. Talk to someone who can guide you. Shame often grows in secrecy, but healing starts with honesty.

Encouragement: Remember 1 Corinthians 10:13, which says that God will provide a way out of temptation. You are not trapped, and there is help available if you ask.

13. Respecting Others' Boundaries and Privacy

It is not just about your own usage. Part of being a good friend and a person of integrity is respecting others online.

- **Ask Before Tagging**: Some friends prefer not to be tagged in photos. Always ask if they are okay with it.
- **Do Not Share Secrets**: If someone tells you something in confidence, do not post about it or forward their messages without permission.
- **Avoid Oversharing About Friends**: Even if you want to express love for a friend, be mindful of how much you reveal. Some details are best kept between you.

Practical Action: If a friend's photo is unflattering or reveals personal info (like a house address in the background), be considerate. You can blur the background or ask them how they feel about posting it.

---

14. Building a Positive Online Identity

Developing a Positive Online Identity
Your online identity is part of who you are. It should reflect your faith, personality, and kindness in a real way.

- **Highlight Good Things**: Share stories or verses that inspire. Show gratitude for small blessings in your life.
- **Keep It Real**: Authenticity means showing that you have ups and downs, not just a perfect image. You do not have to post every failure, but you can be genuine.
- **Spread Good Will**: Use your platform to stand up for kind causes, support friends' projects, or raise awareness for positive efforts.

Seldom Mentioned Benefit: A consistent, respectful online presence can open doors. You never know who might notice your posts or remember your kind words. Opportunities can come from people who see you standing for good things online.

---

15. Involving God in Your Digital Choices

God cares about every area of your life, including how you spend time online. Inviting Him into your digital habits can transform the way you see technology.

- **Pray Before Browsing**: This might seem unusual, but a short prayer like, "God, guide me to use my time wisely" can shift your attitude.
- **Seek Guidance**: If you're not sure if a show, game, or account is appropriate, ask God for wisdom.
- **Ask for Strength**: If you are fighting temptation or negative influences online, ask God to help you resist.

Deep Reflection: Remember that faith is not limited to church or youth group. God's truths apply just as much online as they do offline.

---

16. How to Respond to Online Trends

Trends pop up all the time. Some are harmless, but others can be rude, dangerous, or unkind. As a Christian teen, how do you decide whether to join in?

- **Check the Trend's Nature**: Does it disrespect others, encourage unhealthy behavior, or contradict your values? If yes, skip it.
- **Think Long-Term**: A trend might be popular now, but your posts or videos can remain online forever. Consider whether you will be proud of it later.
- **Create Good Trends**: You could start a wholesome challenge or project that encourages people to do acts of kindness.

Rare Approach: Some teens invite friends to a positive challenge, such as reading a chapter of Proverbs and posting a short reflection. This stands out in a world of often meaningless or harmful online trends.

---

17. Recognizing and Avoiding Online Arguments

Social media is full of heated debates on everything from politics to personal beliefs. Engaging in arguments can sap your energy and sour your spirit.

- **Pick Your Battles**: Not every comment requires a response. You do not have to fix every incorrect statement.
- **Stay Respectful**: If you do enter a discussion, keep your tone polite and focus on facts rather than personal attacks.
- **Know When to Step Back**: If a conversation becomes hateful or unproductive, it is wise to walk away.

Important Thought: Proverbs 15:1 says a gentle answer turns away anger. You can still stand for truth, but do so with kindness and wisdom.

18. Helping Friends with Their Tech Struggles

You might see friends battling screen addiction, online drama, or harmful content. If they seek your help, here are things you can do:

1. **Offer Non-Judgmental Support**: Listen first. Try not to shame them.
2. **Suggest Resources**: Recommend accountability apps, Christian counselors, or helpful articles.
3. **Be a Good Example**: Show them how you handle technology with discipline. They might be inspired to try the same.

Note of Caution: Do not force your advice on someone who is not ready to change. You can plant good ideas and pray for them, but each person has to make the choice themselves.

---

19. Practical Tips to Keep Technology in Its Place

Here are a few direct steps to maintain control over your digital life:

- **Turn Off Notifications**: You do not need a beep every time someone posts or likes something. This reduces distraction.
- **Designate Phone-Free Activities**: For example, keep your phone off when you study, have family meals, or attend church.
- **Use an Alarm Clock**: Rather than relying on your phone's alarm, get a small alarm clock. This way, you are not tempted to scroll first thing in the morning.
- **Regular Digital Detox**: Choose one day a week or one weekend a month to stay offline, if possible. Focus on real-world interactions, reading, or outdoor fun.

Hidden Benefit: A digital detox can refresh your mind and allow you to reconnect with God and loved ones more deeply. You might find you sleep better and feel more at peace afterward.

20. Conclusion and Next Steps

Technology is a powerful tool that can connect, teach, and inspire. It can also drain time, lead to comparison, and introduce harmful content. The key is not to avoid it entirely, but to use it in a way that reflects your faith and respects your well-being.

Questions for Reflection

1. Which apps or sites take up most of your time, and do they help or hurt your spiritual and mental health?
2. Can you think of one boundary you need to set to keep your online usage balanced?
3. How might you use social media to shine a light for Christ?

Practical Action Point
Pick one strategy from this chapter—like turning off certain notifications or setting a "no-phone time" before bed—and put it into action for one week. Note any changes in your mood, concentration, or spiritual focus. If you see positive results, keep going and add more boundaries or healthy habits as needed.

CHAPTER 6

Standing Up for Your Values

Introduction
Living as a Christian teenager can sometimes feel like a tug-of-war. You have peers telling you one thing, media telling you another, and then your faith guiding you in a different direction. Standing up for Christian values does not mean you are perfect, but it does mean you aim to live in a way that reflects God's standards.

This chapter will help you learn how to handle social pressure, criticism, or even ridicule for your beliefs. By the end of it, you will have practical methods and a deeper understanding of what it means to stand firm in faith without being unkind or self-righteous.

---

1. Knowing Your Core Values

Before you can stand up for your values, you need to know what those values are. These could be honesty, purity, respect for authority, kindness, modesty, and so forth. Identifying them ahead of time helps you act rather than react when faced with tough choices.

- **Write Them Down**: List the values that matter most to you as a Christian.
- **Find Biblical Support**: Look for verses that back up these values. This builds confidence in why you hold them.
- **Internal Agreement**: Make sure you genuinely believe these values, rather than just following what others tell you.

Rare Tip: Some teens create a "personal values statement," a short note that sums up their key principles. You can keep it in your phone or journal for quick reminders.

2. Learning to Say "No"

Sometimes, the biggest test of faith is simply saying "no" to something that goes against what you believe. It might be an invitation to a party where harmful substances will be present, or a suggestion from friends to cheat on a test.

- **Be Direct**: A clear, calm "I'm not comfortable with that" is often more effective than making excuses.
- **Offer an Alternative**: If your friends want to hang out in a questionable way, suggest something else that does not violate your standards.
- **Practice Short Phrases**: "No thanks," "I'm good," or "That's not my thing." Having a few prepared lines can help you stand firm in the moment.

Deep Insight: People may respect you more than you think if you say "no" with conviction. Standing your ground can also encourage others who want to avoid wrongdoing but feel too afraid to speak up.

---

3. Dealing with Peer Pressure

Peer pressure is real and can come from close friends or the broader culture. Staying true to your values does not mean you ignore the desire to fit in, but it does mean you refuse to compromise on important matters.

- **Know Your Triggers**: If you often give in to pressure in certain settings—like a friend's house or a school event—prepare yourself mentally before you go.
- **Use a Buddy System**: Find a friend who shares your standards. Team up so you can back each other up in tough situations.
- **Stay Confident**: Even if people tease you, remain calm. Sometimes, bullies back down when they see you are not flustered.

Crucial Reminder: Romans 12:2 advises us not to copy the ways of the world but to let God transform our minds. Peer pressure tries to shape you from the outside, but God's truth shapes you from the inside.

4. Handling Ridicule or Criticism

When you stand up for your values, some people may mock you or call you names like "goody-goody." It can hurt, but there are ways to respond wisely.

- **Stay Respectful**: Do not insult them back. Instead, stay polite or walk away if the conversation is unproductive.
- **Guard Your Heart**: Words can sting. Remind yourself that your true worth comes from God, not from peers.
- **Know When to Laugh It Off**: Sometimes, a calm sense of humor can show that you are not bothered by petty remarks.

Lesser-Known Approach: If someone is repeatedly teasing you about your faith, sometimes having a private, calm talk can help. They might not realize how hurtful their words are. Approaching them kindly and expressing your feelings can lead to a positive change.

---

5. Standing for Kindness in a Harsh World

Standing up for your values is not just about avoiding wrong things. It is also about actively doing right things, like showing kindness in a world where cruelty can be common.

- **Random Acts of Compassion**: Help a classmate struggling with homework, or offer to carry bags for someone who needs assistance.
- **Refuse to Join Gossip**: Gossip can be hurtful. Stand up for the person being talked about or change the topic.
- **Encourage Others**: Write uplifting notes or send thoughtful messages. Let people know they matter.

Rare Angle: Sometimes it's easier to say, "No, I won't do bad things," but it takes extra effort to say, "Yes, I will do good things." Being proactive in kindness is a strong statement of faith.

6. Balancing Humility with Boldness

It is possible to stand up for your values without coming across as prideful. The Bible teaches humility, but it also teaches boldness in faith.

- **Stay Teachable**: Even while standing firm, remember you can learn from others. Being open to respectful conversations shows humility.
- **Acknowledge You Are Not Perfect**: Let people know you struggle too. This helps them see you are not judging them from a high place.
- **Speak Truth Boldly**: When someone directly questions your faith or tries to get you to break your values, speak clearly about what you believe and why.

Practical Wisdom: If you are too timid, you might hide your values. If you are too forceful, people might shut you out. Strive for a balance—kind firmness.

---

7. Using Scripture as Your Foundation

Your values are based on biblical teachings. Knowing and remembering Scripture is crucial for standing strong.

- **Memorize Key Verses**: Pick verses that deal with common challenges you face—temptation, honesty, purity, kindness, etc.
- **Study in Context**: Learning the background of verses can give you deeper insights on how to apply them.
- **Apply What You Read**: It is not enough to know the Bible intellectually. Think about how each verse can guide your daily decisions.

Deep Thought: Jesus used Scripture to resist temptation (Matthew 4:1-11). Following His example can equip you to handle peer pressure or moral dilemmas.

---

8. Identifying Your Strong and Weak Areas

You might be very strong in resisting substance use but weak in standing against gossip. Or you might find it easy to be honest but struggle with online temptations. Recognizing these areas helps you focus your efforts.

- **Self-Reflection**: Spend some time thinking about where you usually give in.
- **Ask for Honest Feedback**: Sometimes a close friend or family member can see your weak areas more clearly than you can.
- **Set Specific Goals**: If gossip is your weakness, decide that when gossip starts, you will either change the subject or walk away.

Rarely Mentioned Fact: Being honest with yourself about your failings is a mark of true maturity. It allows you to invite God's help and grow stronger.

9. Handling Friendships That Clash with Your Values

You might have friends you really care about, but they often encourage things you know are not right. Deciding how to proceed can be difficult.

- **Talk Openly**: Sometimes, friends do not realize they are pressuring you. Let them know how you feel.
- **Set Boundaries**: If they continue pushing harmful behaviors, reduce the time you spend with them.
- **Pray for Them**: You can still care about them from a distance. Ask God to touch their hearts and show them a better path.

Seldom Discussed Idea: You can love a person without approving of their choices. This might mean you keep the friendship but refuse to join in activities that violate your beliefs.

10. Making Tough Decisions Publicly

Sometimes, you might have to make hard choices in front of many people—like refusing to participate in a rude prank at school or declining an event that goes against your faith.

- **Prepare in Advance**: If you know a situation is coming, plan what you will say and do.

- **Stand with Confidence**: People notice quiet confidence. You do not have to make a scene, but do not hide or shrink back.
- **Stay Calm If Challenged**: Others might question your decision. Politely explain your reasoning if you choose, but do not feel obligated to debate if they just want to argue.

Encouragement: These public moments can feel scary, but they also strengthen your character and inspire others. You might be surprised how many people are secretly relieved to see someone stand for good values.

---

11. Using Wise Language

When you defend your beliefs, how you say things matters as much as what you say.

- **Use "I" Statements**: "I believe," or "I feel" can soften the conversation, making it less confrontational.
- **Stay Polite**: Avoid yelling, name-calling, or mocking.
- **Focus on Solutions**: If a situation involves wrongdoing, suggest a better course of action. This shows you are not just complaining but offering answers.

Practical Note: You can say something like, "I really appreciate our friendship, but I am not okay with talking badly about others. Can we talk about something positive instead?"

---

12. Developing Backbone Through Small Choices

Standing up for big values often begins with smaller everyday decisions. Each time you choose to do the right thing, you build moral "muscle."

- **Be Honest in Small Matters**: If a cashier gives you too much change, give it back. Honesty in little things prepares you for bigger moral tests.
- **Keep Promises**: Even if it's inconvenient, doing what you said you would do shows you value truthfulness.

- **Speak Up Early**: If you notice a minor wrongdoing, address it right away. Waiting too long can make it harder to confront.

Advanced Thought: Like physical exercise, moral courage grows with regular practice. The more you stand up for what is right, the stronger you become.

---

13. Turning Mistakes Into Lessons

We all slip up. Maybe you caved to peer pressure or lied to fit in. The important part is what you do afterward.

- **Admit the Failure**: Acknowledge it to yourself and to God.
- **Seek Forgiveness**: If you hurt someone, apologize sincerely.
- **Learn and Move On**: Identify how you ended up slipping. Plan ways to avoid the same trap next time.

Hopeful Reminder: God's grace allows you to start fresh. Mistakes do not disqualify you from being a faithful Christian. They can actually deepen your understanding of how much you need God.

---

14. Finding Support in Community

You do not have to stand for your values alone. Surround yourself with people who share or respect your beliefs.

- **Church Groups**: A youth group or Bible study can provide moral support and friendship.
- **Family**: If your family also holds Christian values, lean on them when you feel pressured or confused.
- **Christian Mentors**: Adults like pastors, Sunday school teachers, or older friends in the faith can guide you with their experience.

Rare Benefit: Being part of a strong Christian community can reduce the sense of isolation. Knowing others believe what you do and have faced similar struggles can motivate you to stay strong.

15. Standing for Truth in Online Spaces

We have already looked at healthy social media use, but sometimes you will face moral issues online. You might see hateful posts, bullying, or misleading information.

- **Respond with Love**: If you decide to comment, do so kindly and respectfully.
- **Limit Arguments**: Online fights rarely lead to real change. Sometimes, leaving a gracious comment or a factual correction is enough.
- **Be an Example**: Your own posts can reflect honesty and positivity. Others might notice and follow suit.

Hidden Thought: Even though online interactions feel less personal, they can have a big impact. Your calm, faith-based approach could influence someone silently watching.

---

16. Guarding Against Self-Righteousness

Standing up for your values is not about looking down on others or acting superior. It is about honoring God and living by His standards.

- **Stay Humble**: Acknowledge that you too need God's grace.
- **Offer Hope, Not Judgment**: If someone is living in a way you do not agree with, show compassion and offer prayer instead of harsh criticism.
- **Be Willing to Listen**: Sometimes people have reasons for their choices. Listening to understand can lead to meaningful discussions.

Balanced View: Jesus spoke truth but was also known for mercy. Aim to do the same. Standing firm without love can push people away from God rather than draw them closer.

---

17. Standing for Purity

Purity is a common area where Christian teens face pressure. This includes purity in your thoughts, body, and relationships.

- **Know Your Boundaries**: Decide in advance what you will or will not do physically or mentally.
- **Share Boundaries with a Trusted Friend**: They can help you stay on track and offer advice when you face temptation.
- **Pray for Strength**: Ask God daily to guide your actions and keep your mind clean.

Seldom Mentioned Detail: Purity is not just about physical behavior; it is also about the media you consume, the jokes you laugh at, and the conversations you engage in. Keeping a pure heart influences every part of your life.

---

18. Influencing Others Positively

When you stand up for values, you might become a role model. Even if you do not see yourself as a leader, your actions and words can quietly shape others.

- **Lead by Example**: People watch what you do more than what you say.
- **Offer Guidance**: If a younger student or a friend asks for help, share what you have learned about maintaining values.
- **Support Others Who Stand for What's Right**: Applaud classmates who refuse to cheat or show kindness to those in need. Standing together is powerful.

Unexpected Effect: Sometimes, classmates who never said anything about faith might approach you privately, thanking you for living by your beliefs. Your silent witness can open doors to deeper conversations.

---

19. Learning from Biblical Heroes

The Bible is full of stories of people who stood firm despite difficulties. For instance:

- **Daniel**: He refused to eat the king's food that went against his faith. Later, he stood strong in prayer even when threatened with a lions' den.
- **Esther**: She risked her life to speak up for her people.
- **Shadrach, Meshach, and Abednego**: They chose not to bow to an idol, even when faced with a fiery furnace.

Reading these stories can inspire you to be brave and trust God in your own situations.

---

20. Walking Forward with Confidence

Standing up for your values as a Christian teen can be challenging, but it is also rewarding. You grow in character, strengthen your faith, and set an example for others.

Questions for Reflection

1. Which Christian value do you find hardest to keep under peer pressure, and why?
2. Who in your life can support you when you feel alone in standing for your beliefs?
3. How will you react next time someone challenges your values?

Practical Action Point

This week, choose one situation where you normally struggle to stand for your values—maybe gossip at lunch or giving in to negative talk online. Plan a clear way to act differently. It could be a simple refusal to join in or offering a better alternative. Afterward, note how it felt and what you learned.

CHAPTER 7

Growing Through Hard Times

Introduction
Everyone goes through difficult moments. As a Christian teen girl, you may have faced situations like grief over losing a loved one, struggling with a health issue, failing a class, or feeling crushed by disappointment. During times of hardship, it can be tempting to feel abandoned or wonder why God allows such difficulties. But these challenges do not have to break you. They can help you grow stronger if you approach them with wisdom and lean on your faith.

In this chapter, we will look at why bad things can happen, how to respond wisely, and how to keep your faith strong despite the storms. You will learn tips that go beyond the usual advice, along with clear examples of how hard times can produce resilience and deepen your trust in God.

---

1. Understanding Hard Times from a Christian Viewpoint

Some people assume that being a Christian means life will be smooth and problem-free. This is not true. Even faithful believers experience pain, loss, and struggles. The Bible contains many stories of godly people who had major hardships. For example, Job lost his health, wealth, and family, yet he continued to seek God. Joseph was sold into slavery by his own brothers, then wrongly jailed, but he still relied on the Lord.

Key Truth: Hard times are often part of living in a broken world. They do not necessarily mean God is punishing you. Rather, God can use them to shape your character, test your faith, and even help you grow in ways you did not think possible.

---

2. Recognizing the Types of Hard Times Teens Face

Your difficulties may look different from those of other teens. Recognizing the type of hardship can help you find the right steps to handle it:

1. **Family Problems**: Divorce, constant arguments, or financial troubles at home can cause stress.
2. **Health Challenges**: Physical illnesses, mental health issues, or injuries can disrupt your normal life.
3. **Academic Setbacks**: Failing a test, not getting into a certain club, or receiving lower grades than expected can feel discouraging.
4. **Social Issues**: Bullying, exclusion, gossip, and changing friendships are common sources of pain.
5. **Personal Grief**: Losing a loved one or even a cherished pet can trigger sadness and confusion.

Rarely Discussed Aspect: A hidden layer of hardship comes from spiritual stress—times when you feel far from God or question your purpose. Recognizing this can be important for finding healing.

---

3. Practical Ways to Find Strength and Comfort

When hard times hit, you might feel overwhelmed or powerless. But there are practical actions that can bring relief and hope:

- **Talk to Someone You Trust**: This could be a parent, counselor, youth leader, or close friend. Sharing your thoughts can help lighten the load.
- **Seek Professional Help**: If the issue is severe—like depression, deep anxiety, or trauma—talk to a mental health professional who respects your faith background.
- **Use Healthy Outlets**: Activities like painting, writing, or playing an instrument can ease tension. They let you express feelings in a safe way.
- **Stay Connected to Supportive People**: Surround yourself with those who pray for you, speak words of kindness, and encourage you to keep going.

Hidden Tip: When a problem seems huge, break it down into smaller parts. For example, if you are failing in math, first talk to the teacher or get a tutor, rather than letting panic overwhelm you.

4. Relying on God's Word

Reading the Bible is not just a religious duty. It can be a source of strength in tough times. Psalms, in particular, contain heartfelt cries from people in distress, showing that God listens even when we feel hurt.

- **Find Specific Passages**: Look for verses that match your situation. If you are worried, read Matthew 6:25-34 about not being anxious. If you are sad, check Psalm 34:18, which says God is close to the brokenhearted.
- **Reflect on God's Promises**: Remind yourself that God is faithful and has good plans for you (Jeremiah 29:11). Repeat His promises to yourself often.
- **Journal Your Thoughts**: Write down the verses that mean the most to you and note how you feel as you read them.

Deeper Thought: The Bible is full of accounts of how God delivered people from tough situations or guided them through. Reflecting on those stories can help you see that your hardship is not the end—it is a stage, and God is with you.

5. Handling Emotional Pain in a Godly Way

Hard times usually bring strong emotions, such as anger, sadness, or worry. God does not want you to ignore these feelings. Instead, He wants you to bring them to Him.

- **Allow Yourself to Feel**: It is okay to cry or express grief. Denying emotions can lead to more stress.
- **Pray Honestly**: Tell God exactly how you feel. If you are disappointed or upset, say so in your prayers. He already knows your heart, and honest prayer can bring relief.
- **Stay Away from Harmful Coping**: Avoid turning to drugs, self-harm, or destructive relationships to numb the pain. These only create bigger problems.
- **Consider Christian Counseling**: A counselor who understands biblical principles can give coping tools for your emotional struggles.

Rarely Mentioned Encouragement: The book of Lamentations shows that it is possible to cry out to God when life feels broken. It is not a sin to weep or feel sorrow. What matters is that you bring those emotions to Him for healing.

6. Using Challenges to Build Endurance

One benefit of facing hard times is that they can build endurance. Just like muscles grow when lifted against resistance, your spiritual and emotional strength can grow when you face problems.

- **Look for Small Wins**: Even small successes, like finishing an assignment during a tough week, can show you that you are capable.
- **Speak Positive Truths**: Say affirmations from the Bible to yourself: "I can do all things through Christ who strengthens me" (Philippians 4:13).
- **Track Your Growth**: Keep a note of how you handled challenges in the past. Did you learn something new about patience, forgiveness, or resilience? This record can motivate you when you face future difficulties.

Advanced Tip: You can use difficult times to develop qualities like compassion and empathy. Once you have faced certain hardships, you can better relate to others going through similar issues.

7. Trusting God's Timing

Many teens wish their problems would disappear instantly. Yet sometimes, God allows a season of waiting or ongoing struggle. This can shape your character and teach you lessons that quick fixes never could.

- **Practice Patience**: Remind yourself that God sees the entire picture of your life. You only see a small part.
- **Stay Faithful in the Wait**: Keep praying, reading Scripture, and doing what you can, even if you see no immediate change.
- **Do Not Compare**: It is easy to look at friends who seem to have an easier life. But each person's path is unique. Focus on your relationship with God.

Unique Thought: Delays can sometimes protect you from an outcome you are not ready for. Trusting God's timing means accepting that sometimes He answers with "Not yet," or "I have something better planned."

---

8. Serving Others During Your Own Hard Time

It might sound surprising, but serving others when you are struggling can actually lighten your own stress. Helping a friend or volunteering at a local shelter can switch your focus from your problems to a larger viewpoint.

- **Small Acts**: Even sending a kind message to someone or praying for a friend can shift your attitude from sadness to compassion.
- **Group Projects**: Join your church or youth group in a service project. Being part of something that brings hope can give you purpose.
- **Be Open About Your Story**: If you feel comfortable, share your experiences with a friend who is also hurting. You could find that your words of empathy bring healing both to them and you.

Deep Reasoning: In 2 Corinthians 1:3-4, it explains that God comforts us in our hardships so we can comfort others in theirs. Your problems can become a bridge to help others see God's goodness.

---

9. Avoiding Bitterness and Self-Pity

It is normal to feel frustrated when life seems unfair. However, staying in anger or self-pity can make you feel stuck. Instead, consider ways to move forward with a healthier perspective:

- **Check Your Heart**: Regularly ask God to reveal if you are harboring bitterness toward a person or situation.
- **Practice Forgiveness**: This does not mean you accept wrong actions, but it frees you from carrying grudges.
- **Write a Gratitude List**: Focusing on what you do have—like supportive friends, a home, food, or any positive aspect—can slowly shift your mood.

Rarely Emphasized Idea: Holding on to bitterness can harm your health and relationships. Forgiveness and choosing gratitude require effort, but they let God's peace have room in your life.

---

10. Learning from Biblical Figures Who Overcame

The Bible is packed with individuals who faced challenges but emerged stronger in faith. Studying their stories can offer life-changing insights:

1. **Ruth**: A young widow who chose to stay with her mother-in-law. Despite losing her husband, she stayed faithful and found a new life and blessing.
2. **David**: He faced a giant named Goliath and many other threats, yet his trust in God helped him become a great king.
3. **Paul**: He was imprisoned many times but continued to preach and wrote much of the New Testament while in chains.

Practical Step: Try doing a short Bible study on one of these figures. Write down the challenges they faced, their response, and how God helped them. Then note how you can apply the same principles.

---

11. Building a Support Network

During hard times, isolation can worsen your pain. It helps to have supportive people around you:

- **Mentors**: A pastor, youth leader, or older relative can offer wisdom.
- **Close Friends**: Seek out friends who respect your faith and can provide prayer and understanding.
- **Therapists or Counselors**: A professional can guide you through specific challenges, whether emotional or mental.
- **Prayer Partners**: Someone who consistently prays for you can become a source of strength.

Rare Tip: Try not to keep your struggles a secret. The body of Christ is meant to uplift one another. Even if it feels scary to share, a caring network can help you feel less alone.

12. Recognizing When You Need Extra Help

Some hardships can be too big to face with prayer and general support alone—especially if you are dealing with ongoing depression, trauma, or harmful behaviors.

- **Warning Signs**: If you feel hopeless, think about harming yourself, or cannot carry out everyday tasks, seek immediate help from a trusted adult.
- **Talk Openly**: Speak to a teacher, counselor, doctor, or church leader. They can guide you to resources like therapy, support groups, or in some cases, medication.
- **Know It Is Not a Lack of Faith**: Using professional help does not mean you lack trust in God. It means you are being wise about your well-being.

Important Note: Churches sometimes have partnerships with Christian counseling centers. Do not hesitate to ask your youth pastor or church office if they can refer you to someone who aligns with your beliefs.

13. Releasing the Past and Looking Ahead

Hard times can leave scars. You might be tempted to replay the past in your mind. However, dwelling too much on past pain can block your future growth.

- **Give Yourself Time to Heal**: Healing is a process. Give yourself patience as you work through emotions.
- **Release Shame**: If you made mistakes during hard times, remember that God offers forgiveness. You do not have to stay locked in regret.
- **Set New Goals**: Looking forward to new goals—be it academic, personal, or spiritual—can reignite hope.

Advanced Thought: Writing a "future hope list" can help. Write down dreams you have or positive changes you want to see. Pray over them regularly, asking God for guidance and motivation.

14. Reminding Yourself of God's Goodness

It can be easy to forget God's goodness when in pain. One way to push back against hopelessness is to remember all the blessings God has poured out on you in the past.

- **Testimony Journal**: Keep a record of answered prayers or moments when you felt God's guidance. Reread these entries during low points.
- **Praise Playlist**: Gather worship songs that remind you of God's nature—His love, mercy, and power. Listen to them often.
- **Nature Walk**: Observing God's creation, like the sky, trees, or small animals, can remind you that He is still in control.

Unique Strategy: Some people place sticky notes of Bible verses or short prayers around their room. This way, they see reminders of God's goodness throughout the day.

---

15. Gaining Wisdom and Compassion

Difficult seasons can teach you lessons about life, faith, and relationships that you might not have learned otherwise.

- **Mature Perspective**: You realize what truly matters versus what is trivial.
- **Empathy**: Having been through challenges yourself, you become more sensitive to the needs of others.
- **Reliance on God**: Struggles can strip away pride, causing you to lean on God more. This results in deeper faith.

Rare Benefit: Sometimes, facing a hard time helps you discover gifts you did not know you had—like a talent for comforting others, a knack for problem-solving, or a creative skill that emerges as you cope.

---

16. Offering Forgiveness to Yourself and Others

Sometimes hard times involve mistakes you made or wrongs done by someone else. Holding grudges can lock you in bitterness, while refusing to forgive yourself can lead to shame.

- **Reflect on God's Forgiveness**: Remember that if God can forgive you, you can forgive yourself.
- **Set Boundaries if Needed**: Forgiving someone does not mean you allow them to keep hurting you. You can forgive while still maintaining distance if it is safer for you.
- **Ask God for Strength**: True forgiveness can be hard. You may need to pray often for a heart that is willing to release resentment.

Advanced Tip: If you are stuck in a cycle of guilt, talk to a pastor or mentor about it. Sometimes speaking it out and receiving gentle guidance can free you from the weight.

---

17. Honoring God in the Storm

Faith does not mean ignoring pain or pretending everything is okay. It means deciding that no matter what happens, you will honor God's name and hold on to His truth.

- **Live with Integrity**: Continue to do what is right, even if your situation is not improving.
- **Offer Praise in Difficulty**: Singing or praying praises to God when you are hurting can be a profound act of faith.
- **Stay Committed**: Keep attending church, youth group, or Bible study even when you feel sad. This helps you remain anchored.

Biblical Inspiration: Paul and Silas praised God in prison (Acts 16:25). Their circumstances were grim, but they still worshiped. Their example shows that real faith endures, even when everything seems against you.

---

18. Guarding Against Despair

Hard times can push you to the edge of despair, leading you to lose hope or feel that life is meaningless. If you feel yourself heading in that direction, remember these points:

- **You Are Not Alone**: Many people in the Bible and in history have walked through dark valleys and found a fresh start.
- **Your Pain Is Valid**: It is okay to admit you feel terrible. Denying it often makes it worse.
- **Help Is Available**: Counseling, prayer, and medical help can turn things around. Do not give up before you seek real solutions.

Reminder: Psalm 30:5 says, "Weeping may last through the night, but joy comes with the morning." This verse does not promise that hardships will vanish quickly, but it does show that a brighter day can come if you do not lose heart.

---

19. Sharing Your Story for God's Glory

Overcoming hard times can become part of your testimony. By sharing what God brought you through, you encourage others to trust Him with their own problems.

- **Opportunities to Share**: It could be at youth group, a social media post (used wisely), or a heart-to-heart conversation with a friend.
- **Be Honest**: You do not need to pretend you had it all together. Sharing your struggles and how you found strength points to God's grace.
- **Inspire Hope**: Your story might be the very thing another teen needs to hear so they do not give up.

Careful Balance: When sharing publicly, be mindful of personal details. You can be open about your journey without exposing everything if it is sensitive. Always seek God's direction on what to share and when.

---

20. Moving Forward in Strength

Hard times, although painful, can shape you into a person of deep faith, empathy, and resilience. Trust that God holds you in His hands and has a plan that goes beyond your current troubles.

Questions for Reflection

1. What is one lesson you have learned from a hard time you faced?
2. Who can you reach out to for support if you feel overwhelmed?
3. How can you use your experiences to help someone else going through a crisis?

Practical Action Point
Think of a specific challenge you are currently facing. Write down three possible steps you can take (for example, seeking counsel, studying a comforting Bible passage, or talking to a trusted friend). Plan to do at least one of these steps in the next week. Ask God to guide you and provide the courage to act.

Conclusion to Chapter 7
Hard times do not have to crush you. Yes, they can hurt and test your limits, but they also offer a chance to develop greater trust in God and a deeper understanding of His goodness. By seeking helpful resources, being honest with your emotions, and standing firm in your faith, you can find hope in the darkest days. Let these times refine you into a compassionate, sturdy young woman who knows that God is ever-present—even in the storm.

CHAPTER 8

Finding Strength in Prayer

Introduction
Prayer is more than a spiritual ritual. It is a conversation with God that can shape your thoughts, provide comfort, and guide you through decisions. For a Christian teen girl, prayer can be a powerful source of help in daily life—whether you are feeling anxious about school, confused about friendships, or excited about future plans.

In this chapter, we will look at the importance of prayer, different ways to pray, and how to overcome common obstacles. Instead of treating prayer as a dry habit, you will learn how to make it a vital part of your relationship with God.

---

1. Why Prayer Matters

Some people treat prayer like a last resort when things go wrong. However, the Bible tells us to pray continually (1 Thessalonians 5:17). Prayer is an open line of communication with the Creator of the universe.

- **Builds a Closer Bond with God**: When you talk to God often, you learn more about His heart and start seeing your life from His viewpoint.
- **Calms Worries**: Laying your concerns before God can bring peace. Philippians 4:6-7 says that when we pray instead of worrying, God's peace guards our hearts.
- **Opens You to God's Will**: Regular prayer helps you discover where God wants to lead you and how He wants you to act.

Seldom Mentioned Point: Prayer is not about perfect words. It is about sincerity. Even if you are stumbling over your sentences, God listens to the posture of your heart.

---

2. Overcoming Prayer Struggles

Many teens want to pray more but feel stuck. Common obstacles include:

- **Busyness**: School, activities, and chores can eat up your schedule, leaving little time for prayer.
- **Distraction**: In a world full of smartphones and social media, staying focused during prayer can be hard.
- **Uncertainty**: You might not know how to pray or feel like you do not have the right words.
- **Doubt**: You may question whether God is really listening or if prayer makes a difference.

Practical Response: Schedule daily prayer the same way you schedule other important tasks. Find a quiet spot, put your phone aside, and begin with a simple format—like praising God, confessing sins, giving thanks, and presenting requests.

3. Different Types of Prayer

Prayer can take many forms. Exploring these can make your communication with God more meaningful and less repetitive.

1. **Adoration**: Praising God for who He is—His power, love, and holiness. Example: "God, You are awesome and full of mercy."
2. **Confession**: Admitting sins or failures. Example: "Lord, forgive me for losing my temper at my brother."
3. **Thanksgiving**: Expressing gratitude. Example: "Thank You for helping me pass that test."
4. **Supplication**: Asking for God's help for yourself or others. Example: "Please guide my friend who is having a tough time at home."

Tip for Teens: A simple memory aid is "ACTS"—Adoration, Confession, Thanksgiving, Supplication. This can help you remember to pray in a balanced way instead of only asking for things.

4. Setting Up a Consistent Prayer Routine

When you are trying to build a habit of prayer, consistency is key. But it does not have to be complicated.

- **Morning Check-In**: Say a brief prayer when you first wake up. Dedicate your day to God, asking Him to guide you in decisions and attitudes.
- **Midday Pause**: If possible, take a moment during lunch or a break at school to say a short prayer. Thank God for what has happened so far and ask for help with the rest of the day.
- **Evening Reflection**: Before bed, review your day. Confess any sins, thank God for blessings, and bring your requests to Him.

Rare Strategy: Some teens set alarms on their phone to remind them to pray at certain times. Each alarm can have a short note like "Time to talk to God." This creates a gentle nudge to pause and connect.

---

5. Praying Through Scripture

Reading Scripture alongside your prayers can deepen your understanding of God's promises and help you pray in alignment with His Word.

- **Pick a Passage**: Choose a section of the Bible—maybe a Psalm or a few verses from the Gospels.
- **Reflect and Pray**: After reading, talk to God about what you learned. If the passage mentions God's power, praise Him for that power in your life.
- **Personalize the Text**: For instance, if you read Psalm 23, pray something like, "God, be my shepherd today. Lead me to good decisions and protect me from harm."

Seldom Talked About Angle: You can pray entire Bible verses verbatim, turning them into personal requests or praises. This can boost your confidence that you are praying according to God's truth.

6. Praying with Friends or Family

Prayer does not have to be a solo activity. Group prayer can strengthen relationships and create unity.

- **Family Prayer Time**: Suggest praying together at dinner or before bedtime. Each family member can share one prayer request and one praise.
- **Prayer Partners**: Find a friend who also wants to grow in faith. You can meet weekly or exchange messages with prayer requests.
- **Small Group Sessions**: If you are part of a youth group or Bible study, suggest a short prayer circle. Hearing each other's needs encourages you to support each other better.

Hidden Gem: Group prayer helps you learn from others' prayer styles. You might pick up new ways of praising God or addressing life's problems that you had not considered before.

---

7. Finding the Right Environment

Where you pray can influence your focus and openness:

- **Quiet Corner**: A small area in your room or another private spot where you can kneel or sit without distractions.
- **Nature Walk**: Some teens feel closer to God outdoors. You could walk in a park, observing creation while praying silently.
- **Church Sanctuary**: If your church is open during the week, sitting quietly in the sanctuary can foster a sense of reverence.

Practical Idea: If you are an active person, you can pray while doing light exercise. A slow jog or a relaxed walk can pair well with silent or whispered prayer, as long as you are safe and alert to your surroundings.

8. Handling Unanswered Prayers

One of the toughest challenges in prayer is feeling like God is not answering. You might pray for a specific outcome, only to see no clear response.

- **Check Your Motives**: Sometimes we pray for things that might not be best for us, or we pray with a selfish outlook. James 4:3 warns that wrong motives can hinder prayers.
- **God's Timing**: Delays do not always mean denial. As discussed in previous chapters, God's timetable can be different from ours.
- **Look for Subtle Answers**: God might be answering in ways you did not expect—by changing your heart, opening a different door, or sending support through a friend.

Hopeful Perspective: Sometimes a "no" from God protects you from a greater harm. Other times, a "wait" builds your patience and teaches you deeper trust.

---

9. Learning to Listen

Prayer is not just talking; it is also listening. You can miss God's gentle guidance if you are always speaking and never pausing to hear Him.

- **Be Still**: After you pray, remain quiet for a couple of minutes. This can feel awkward at first, but it trains you to be open to God's inner promptings.
- **Pay Attention to Impressions**: Thoughts or ideas might pop into your mind that align with God's Word and your situation. Test them against Scripture and wise counsel.
- **Journaling**: Write down what you sense God might be saying. Over time, you can see patterns of how He leads you.

Encouraging Note: Listening does not usually involve hearing an audible voice. Often, God speaks through the Bible, through people you trust, or through a gentle nudge in your heart.

10. Praying in Tough Moments

It is easy to pray when life is calm, but what about when you are upset, worried, or facing sudden challenges?

- **Emergency Prayers**: A quick "God, help me" in the middle of a crisis can be powerful. God does not need fancy words to act.
- **Scripture-Filled Declarations**: If fear strikes, say verses out loud. This builds faith and pushes back panic.
- **Worship as Prayer**: Sometimes, putting on a worship song and singing along can become a direct prayer to God in moments of stress.

Example: If you are suddenly overwhelmed by social anxiety, try stepping away quietly, breathe deeply, and pray: "Lord, be my peace right now." Then recall a verse about God's peace, such as John 14:27.

---

11. Using Prayer to Guide Decisions

Prayer is not just for emotional comfort. It is also key when you face decisions about friendships, relationships, college, or everyday choices.

- **Ask for Wisdom**: James 1:5 promises that God gives wisdom to those who ask for it.
- **Look for Confirmation**: After praying, see if Scripture, advice from godly people, or circumstances point in the same direction.
- **Keep an Open Mind**: Sometimes, God's answer might surprise you. Stay willing to follow, even if it is not your initial preference.

Deep Thought: Large life decisions can be less scary when you trust that God is directing you. This does not remove personal responsibility, but it ensures you do not rely on your own understanding alone.

---

12. Thanking God After Answers

When you finally receive an answer—whether it is a clear yes, no, or a changed heart—remember to give thanks. Too often, we pray earnestly but forget to show gratitude when the solution comes.

- **Thank-You Journal**: Keep a record of answered prayers. Reflect on how God has been faithful.
- **Share the Good News**: Telling a friend or family member how God answered your prayer can build their faith as well.
- **Continue Praying**: Do not stop connecting with God just because your crisis is over. Keep building the relationship.

Hidden Advantage: Practicing gratitude keeps you aware of God's presence in every part of your life. It also brings joy and humility, reminding you that all good things come from Him.

---

13. Dealing with Guilt That Blocks Prayer

Sometimes, you might avoid prayer because you feel ashamed over sin or mistakes. You worry that God is angry or disappointed. However, the Bible teaches that Jesus came to bring forgiveness.

- **Acknowledge Sin**: Do not hide from it. Confess it openly in prayer. 1 John 1:9 says that if we confess our sins, God will forgive us and purify us.
- **Accept Forgiveness**: Believing in God's grace frees you from condemnation. You do not have to be perfect before you pray; approach God with a humble heart.
- **Move Forward**: True repentance means turning away from the wrongdoing, but you can still come to God as you work through that process.

Seldom Addressed Truth: Guilt can become a chain that the enemy uses to stop you from praying. Breaking free by confessing and accepting forgiveness is a key step to restoring that connection with God.

---

14. Learning from Praying People in the Bible

Scripture shows many examples of people who prayed with remarkable outcomes:

- **Hannah**: She prayed desperately for a child, and God granted her request (1 Samuel 1).
- **Elijah**: His prayers led to miracles, like stopping rain for three years, then praying again and rain fell (1 Kings 17-18).
- **Daniel**: Even under threat of death, he prayed faithfully three times a day (Daniel 6).

Suggestion: Pick one biblical figure known for prayer and study their life. Notice what they asked God for, how they prayed, and the results they saw. This can motivate you to pray with more conviction.

---

15. Keeping Your Mind from Wandering

Many people struggle with random thoughts invading their mind when trying to pray. This is normal. Here are tips to stay on track:

- **Use a Prayer List**: Write down prayer points. As you pray, follow the list to maintain focus.
- **Pray Aloud**: Speaking your prayers can hold your attention better than silent thoughts.
- **Keep a Pen and Paper Handy**: If a random task comes to mind, jot it down quickly and return to prayer. That way, you won't forget it, but it also won't derail your prayer time.

Small Trick: Some teens find it helpful to pace around a room while praying quietly out loud. The movement can keep them more alert than sitting still with eyes closed.

---

16. Praying for Others Selflessly

It is easy to focus prayers on your own needs. However, God calls us to pray for others too.

- **Friends and Family**: Lift up their struggles and successes, asking God to guide and bless them.
- **Global Issues**: Pray for people in other countries, especially where Christians face persecution or hardship.

- **Leaders and Authorities**: The Bible suggests praying for those in authority, such as government officials, school principals, and pastors.

Benefit: Praying for others broadens your perspective, fosters compassion, and reminds you that God's plan goes beyond your personal world.

---

17. Avoiding Religious Routine

Prayer can become a mere habit if you are not careful, especially if you just rattle off the same words without meaning. To keep prayer sincere:

- **Vary Your Approach**: Sometimes kneel, sometimes stand, sometimes walk. Change the time or place to keep it fresh.
- **Include Worship Music**: Sing a short chorus or hymn as part of your prayer time.
- **Pause to Listen**: Remember that silence is part of prayer too. That quiet space can let God's peace sink in.

Realistic Insight: Routine can be helpful (like a daily schedule), but never lose the heartfelt connection. Treat prayer as a meeting with a loving Father, not a box to check.

---

18. Using Technology to Strengthen Prayer (Wisely)

We live in a digital age, and you can use technology in good ways to help your prayer life (as explained in Chapter 5 regarding balanced tech use).

- **Prayer Apps**: Some apps send reminders or offer prayer journals and group chats for sharing requests.
- **Online Bible**: Reading a digital Bible and highlighting verses can help you pray with a scriptural focus.
- **Music Platforms**: Create a playlist of worship songs to guide your heart into a state of prayer.

Caution: Make sure these digital tools do not turn into distractions. Once you open your phone, it is easy to check messages or scroll mindlessly. Set a clear purpose before you unlock the screen.

19. Growing in Confidence Through Prayer

As you develop a deeper prayer life, you will likely notice changes:

- **Stronger Faith**: Seeing God answer prayers—even in small ways—builds your confidence that He hears you.
- **Clearer Direction**: When you pray consistently, you become more sensitive to God's leading in daily decisions.
- **Inner Peace**: Rather than bottling up worries, you learn to release them to God. Over time, this brings calmness.

Encouraging Thought: You do not have to be an adult or a pastor to have a strong prayer life. God values the prayers of teens. Your words matter to Him just as much as anyone else's.

20. Moving Forward in Prayer

Prayer is a lifelong practice. It changes as you grow, but it remains a steady thread connecting you to God. You might use different methods over time, but the core principle stays the same: sharing your heart with the One who made you, loves you, and guides you.

Questions for Reflection

1. Which obstacle keeps you from praying more often—distraction, fear, or lack of time?
2. What is one change you can make to set aside dedicated prayer moments each day?
3. How can praying for others expand your compassion and help you see the world as God does?

Practical Action Point
In the next week, try a new prayer method—maybe writing your prayers in a journal, praying with a friend, or praying outside in nature. Take note of how it affects your focus and sense of peace. If you find it helpful, add it to your regular routine.

CHAPTER 9

Exploring Positive Habits

Introduction

Habits shape your everyday life. They guide how you spend your time and how you act, often without much thought. Good habits can boost your health, academic progress, faith, and relationships. Bad habits, however, can hold you back and leave you frustrated. For a Christian teen girl, it is useful to learn how to form positive habits that line up with the values taught in the Bible.

In this chapter, we will look at ways to form good habits, how to break harmful ones, and how faith ties into each step. You will find details on practical planning as well as insights from Scripture. By the end, you will see that small choices every day can lead to big changes that help you stay strong in your Christian walk.

1. Why Habits Matter

Habits are actions you do so often that they become part of your routine. Some are obvious, like brushing your teeth. Others may be less clear, like checking your phone first thing in the morning. The reason habits matter is that they have power to shape who you become. Over time, repeated behaviors can either push you toward your goals or pull you away from them.

- **Impact on Your Mind**: Habits influence how you think. For instance, if you always start your day with a negative thought, it can put you in a bad mood. On the other hand, choosing a grateful mindset first thing can set a positive tone for the rest of your day.
- **Impact on Your Body**: Physical habits—like what you eat, how often you exercise, or your sleep schedule—play a big role in your health and energy.
- **Impact on Your Spirit**: Spiritual habits—like prayer, Bible study, and serving others—can help you grow closer to God.

Seldom Stated Fact: A habit, once formed, can become almost automatic. This means if you build the right habits now, you will benefit from them for years to come without having to push yourself too hard.

2. Identifying Your Current Habits

Before you can build new, positive habits, it helps to take an honest look at the habits you already have. Some might be helping you; some might be holding you back.

1. **Make a List**: Write down your everyday routines. For instance, what do you do in the morning, after school, and at night?
2. **Highlight the Good Ones**: Perhaps you always pray before meals or do your homework right after you get home. These are habits worth keeping.
3. **Note the Harmful Ones**: Maybe you scroll on social media endlessly at bedtime or often skip breakfast. Recognize these patterns so you can work on them.

Practical Step: For a few days, keep a small notebook or a note on your phone. Record anything you notice you do repeatedly—like snacking when bored or complaining when stressed. This will give you a clear starting point.

3. The Power of Small Beginnings

Forming a big, complex habit can feel overwhelming. A better approach is to start small. If you want to read the Bible daily but hardly ever do, it might be too much to jump into reading multiple chapters at once. Instead, you could aim for five minutes of Bible reading each day.

- **Small Action, Big Impact**: A short daily commitment might not seem like much. But over weeks and months, it can become a significant improvement in your spiritual life.
- **Easier to Maintain**: If your goal is too large, you may give up quickly when life gets busy. Smaller habits are more likely to stick.
- **Build Momentum**: Once a small habit becomes part of your routine, you can add a bit more time or depth. Maybe five minutes turns into ten, then fifteen, as you grow more comfortable.

Idea: If you want to exercise regularly, you could start with a simple ten-minute walk each day. Once that feels natural, you can add more challenging workouts or a longer time period.

---

4. Linking a New Habit to an Old One

An effective way to form a new habit is to connect it to something you already do. For example, if you want to memorize Scripture, you might decide to review a verse right after you brush your teeth each morning. Brushing your teeth is the existing habit, and reviewing Scripture is the new habit you attach to it.

- **Identify a Trigger**: Choose a habit you never skip, like making your bed or eating breakfast.
- **Add the New Habit**: Right after or right before that action, do the new behavior.
- **Stay Consistent**: Over time, your brain will expect you to do both, making it easier to remember.

Example: If you always have a cup of tea after school, you might attach a five-minute gratitude reflection to that tea time. You sip your tea, and while you do, you think about three things you are thankful for.

---

5. Breaking Harmful Habits

Stopping a bad habit is often harder than forming a good one, but it is not impossible. Here are steps to consider:

1. **Identify the Cause**: Figure out what triggers the harmful habit. Is it boredom, stress, or peer pressure?
2. **Replace It with Something Good**: Instead of just trying to "stop," choose a healthier action. For instance, if you tend to snack on junk food when you are stressed, you can replace it with doing a quick stretch or writing in a journal instead.
3. **Create Barriers**: Make it tougher to engage in the bad habit. If social media distracts you, delete the app from your phone or set strict screen time limits.

4. **Seek Accountability**: Ask a friend or mentor to check in with you. Knowing someone else will ask about your progress can keep you on track.

Point to Remember: Simply telling yourself to quit is not always enough. You need a plan. Replacing the negative action with a positive one helps fill the gap, making it more likely to succeed.

---

6. Using Scripture for Motivation

The Bible has many verses that speak about diligence, discipline, and living wisely. These can motivate you when you feel like giving up on a habit.

- **2 Timothy 1:7**: Reminds us that God gave us a spirit of power, love, and self-control.
- **Proverbs 6:6-8**: Uses the example of the ant's diligence in storing food, teaching us to be responsible and hardworking.
- **Colossians 3:23**: Tells us to do everything as if we are working for God, which can inspire excellence.

Practical Tip: Write down verses that encourage you to form good habits. Place them where you see them often—on your desk, bathroom mirror, or phone wallpaper. When you feel lazy or tempted to fall into an old pattern, read those verses for a boost of strength.

---

7. Habit Stacking for a Balanced Life

You might feel there are many areas you want to improve: physical fitness, time management, spiritual growth, and so on. Trying to fix everything at once can overwhelm you. Instead, consider a gradual approach called "habit stacking," where you build one habit at a time, then stack another on top once the first is steady.

1. **Pick One Area**: Start with what feels most important right now. If that is spiritual growth, begin with daily prayer or Bible reading.

2. **Set a Simple Goal**: For instance, pray for five minutes each morning. Keep at it until it becomes natural.
3. **Add Another Habit**: Once the first is established, add a second one—like a short workout or writing a gratitude list.
4. **Watch Them Grow**: Over weeks and months, these stacked habits form a strong routine that covers multiple areas of your life.

Seldom Used Example: If your goal is to have a morning routine that lifts your mood, you could stack habits like this:

- Wake up → Drink water → Read a short Bible verse → Stretch for two minutes → Get dressed.

Once this set is ingrained, you can add another layer, like journaling or writing a quick prayer.

---

8. Overcoming Laziness and Procrastination

Many people struggle with putting things off or feeling too lazy to start a new routine. Here are some strategies to push through:

- **Set Short Deadlines**: If you need to read a chapter for school or memorize a Scripture passage, give yourself a deadline. Sometimes, the simple presence of a deadline boosts your drive.
- **Use Visual Reminders**: Keep a calendar or chart to mark each day you follow your habit. Seeing a streak of completed days can encourage you not to break it.
- **Reward Yourself**: After a week of staying on track, treat yourself in a small, healthy way—like a relaxing bubble bath or extra reading time for a favorite book.
- **Manage Time Wisely**: Plan your day in chunks. If you know you have 20 minutes before dinner, use that to work on your new habit. Then you do not have to do it all at once.

Deep Insight: Often, laziness is a mask for lack of clarity or overwhelm. Break big tasks into smaller steps, and you might find you feel less lazy because you know exactly what to do next.

9. The Role of Accountability Partners

Sometimes, having someone who supports your goals can make all the difference. An accountability partner is a person you trust—maybe a friend or an older mentor—who will ask about your progress, encourage you, and keep you motivated.

- **Choose Wisely**: Pick someone who genuinely wants the best for you and will give honest feedback.
- **Set Clear Expectations**: Decide how often you will check in—daily messages, weekly coffee meetups, or phone calls.
- **Celebrate Successes**: When you hit a milestone, rejoice together. This shared positivity keeps you both inspired.
- **Stay Open to Correction**: Your partner might point out if you are slipping. Accept it graciously and adjust your habits as needed.

Note: Peer pressure can be used in a positive way here. If your friend knows you plan to do daily Bible reading, you might feel more motivated to stay on track because you do not want to let them down.

---

10. Balancing Discipline with Grace

Forming positive habits is good, but what happens when you miss a day or slip back into a bad habit? Some people become overly harsh on themselves, leading to discouragement. Balance discipline with grace.

- **Recognize You're Human**: Everyone has off-days. A lapse does not mean you have failed entirely.
- **Pick It Up Again**: If you skip your morning devotion one day, get back to it the next day. You do not have to wait for the next Monday or the next month to start fresh.
- **Learn from Mistakes**: Examine why you slipped up. Were you tired, busy, or distracted? Adjust your plan to avoid the same pitfall.
- **Remember God's Mercy**: Lamentations 3:22-23 says God's mercies are new every morning. If He shows you grace, you can show some grace to yourself as well.

Encouraging Fact: True growth comes with ups and downs. The important part is the overall direction you are heading, not momentary setbacks.

---

11. Healthy Habits for Body and Mind

While spiritual habits are crucial, do not overlook the importance of physical and mental health. Good physical habits can help you stay energized and focused on spiritual matters, too.

- **Sleep Routine**: Aim for 7-9 hours of sleep each night. Your body and mind recover during rest, making you more alert and emotionally stable.
- **Nourishing Foods**: Try to include fruits, vegetables, whole grains, and lean protein. While treats are okay sometimes, too much junk food can affect mood and energy.
- **Regular Movement**: This can be anything from a dance class to a brisk walk. Physical activity helps manage stress and keeps your body strong.
- **Mental Breaks**: Whether it is journaling, coloring, or sitting quietly, taking short breaks can prevent burnout.

Lesser-Known Angle: Keeping your body healthy can actually support your prayer life. When you are tired or unwell, it is harder to focus on spiritual growth. By forming healthy habits, you set yourself up to connect with God more effectively.

---

12. Building Intellectual and Creative Habits

Your mind is also a gift from God. Developing habits that stretch your intellect and creative side can help you discover new talents and interests.

- **Reading Regularly**: It could be Christian books, inspiring biographies, or educational resources. This can open your mind to different perspectives and knowledge.
- **Creative Pursuits**: Writing poems, sketching, crafting, or playing a musical instrument can refresh your mind and reduce stress.

- **Mindful Media Consumption**: Choose uplifting shows, podcasts, or music that help you grow rather than content that wastes your time or pulls you into negative thinking.

Rare Tip: If you feel stuck in a creative habit, try a "creativity timer." Work on your art or writing for a set period—like 15 minutes—each day. This consistent effort often sparks bigger ideas over time.

---

13. Spiritual Habits That Strengthen Your Faith

This book has already covered prayer, Bible reading, and church community. However, there are more spiritual habits that can deepen your relationship with God.

- **Bible Memorization**: Pick a verse each week to memorize. This keeps God's word in your heart even when you do not have a Bible nearby.
- **Fasting**: Some believers practice occasional fasting, giving up a meal or certain foods to focus on prayer. If you are a teen, do this carefully and possibly with guidance from a parent or youth leader.
- **Acts of Service**: Serving others regularly—like volunteering at a food pantry or helping an elderly neighbor—keeps your faith active and shows God's love to the world.
- **Worship and Music**: Setting aside time to sing or listen to worship songs can lift your spirit and remind you of God's presence in daily life.

Hidden Value: These habits not only draw you closer to God but also set an example for friends or siblings. They see your steady commitment and might be inspired to do the same.

---

14. Handling Habit-Related Disappointments

Even if you have the best intentions, you might face disappointments. Maybe you promised yourself you would read one chapter of Proverbs each day, but you keep forgetting. Or you planned to exercise daily but fell behind. Here's how to cope:

- **Forgive Yourself Quickly**: The longer you beat yourself up, the less energy you have to correct course.
- **Adjust Your Plan**: If reading a chapter is too much, try a few verses instead. If daily exercise is tough, aim for three times a week.
- **Talk It Out**: Share your frustration with a friend or mentor. They might have gone through the same struggle and can offer advice.
- **Focus on Progress**: If you used to read the Bible zero times a week and now do it twice, that is still growth. Celebrate small steps forward.

Important Perspective: Habit-building is not a pass-or-fail test. It is a continuous effort that evolves with your life circumstances.

---

15. Recognizing God's Help in Forming Habits

Often, we try to build good habits all by ourselves. While personal discipline is important, believers have the advantage of God's help.

- **Pray for Guidance**: Ask God to show you which habits are most important for you right now.
- **Rely on the Holy Spirit**: The Bible teaches that the Holy Spirit can give us self-control (Galatians 5:22-23). Invite Him to guide and strengthen you each day.
- **Give Thanks**: As you see progress, remember to thank God for empowering you. This keeps you humble and reminds you that He is involved in every part of your life.

Deep Thought: Forming habits can sometimes feel like a self-improvement project, but for a Christian, it is also about honoring God with your time, body, and actions.

---

16. Helping Friends Develop Good Habits

You are not the only one who benefits from positive habits. Friends might notice your changes and want to learn from you. Here's how you can help:

1. **Share Your Experience**: Tell them what worked for you and what did not. Be honest about your struggles.
2. **Suggest Simple Steps**: If they are overwhelmed, encourage them to start small. Offer to do a habit together, like reading a Bible verse daily at the same time.
3. **Pray Together**: This can keep you both accountable and invite God into the process.
4. **Celebrate Their Wins**: If your friend hits a milestone, acknowledge it. Send them a text or give a high-five in person.

Note: Avoid forcing your habits on someone who is not interested. You can be a positive influence without being pushy. Let them see the benefits in your life and decide on their own.

17. Using Tools and Apps Wisely

Technology can be a friend or a foe in forming habits. If used wisely, it can make your journey easier.

- **Habit-Tracking Apps**: There are plenty of apps where you can check off daily tasks, view progress graphs, and even earn fun badges.
- **Reminder Alerts**: Setting alarms or notifications can help you remember your tasks. However, be sure to prevent your phone from becoming a distraction.
- **Digital Devotionals**: Some apps offer daily verses, short lessons, and reflection questions. They can remind you to spend time with God.

Caution: Ensure you do not replace actual commitment with just ticking boxes. The goal is genuine growth, not just collecting digital streaks. Use the tools as helpers, not replacements for heartfelt effort.

18. Celebrating Wins

Marking Milestones
When you successfully stick to a habit for a certain period, it's good to mark that achievement. This positive feedback can motivate you to keep going.

- **Personal Rewards**: This could be a special notebook, a relaxing outing, or trying a new hobby you have been excited about.
- **Share with Your Support Network**: Let your accountability partner or family know you reached a milestone. Let them cheer you on.
- **Reflect on God's Goodness**: Spend time thanking God for helping you stay consistent. Offer a prayer of gratitude, acknowledging His role in your progress.

Rare Approach: Some teens keep a "habit victory jar." Each time they hit a milestone—like a full week of consistent Bible reading—they write it on a slip of paper and drop it in the jar. Over time, the jar fills with reminders of progress and blessings.

---

19. Keeping Habits Alive During Busy Seasons

Life is not always stable. You might face exam weeks, family events, or personal challenges that disrupt your routine. The key is learning to adapt rather than quitting.

- **Scale Down**: If you cannot do your full habit, do a shorter or simpler version. For instance, if you normally pray for ten minutes, do a two-minute focused prayer when extremely busy.
- **Plan Ahead**: Look at your schedule for the week. Identify pockets of time you can still maintain your habit.
- **Stay Flexible**: If you miss a day or two, do not spiral into guilt. Pick it back up as soon as possible.

Encouragement: Habits can be adjusted to fit different life situations. The overall goal remains the same—to grow in a steady, positive direction.

---

20. Moving Forward with Hope

Good habits lead to a better life, but they also deepen your walk with God. As you set healthy patterns for your body, mind, and spirit, you reflect a lifestyle that pleases Him. Rather than feeling trapped by harmful habits or disorganized routines, you can walk with confidence, knowing you are making wise use of your time and abilities.

Questions for Reflection

1. What is one habit you want to start, and how can you break it down into small steps?
2. Do you have any harmful habits that need replacing? Which positive habit can take their place?
3. Who could be your accountability partner to keep you motivated?

Practical Action Point
Pick a new habit you want to form and link it to a habit you already have. Decide on a small, realistic goal. If you want to pray more, choose a time of day when you are sure you can pause, such as right before you sit down for breakfast. Keep track of it for the next two weeks, and be prepared to adjust if needed.

Conclusion to Chapter 9
Building positive habits is one of the best ways to grow into a mature and balanced person. By starting small, attaching new habits to existing routines, and relying on both personal discipline and God's help, you can make lasting changes. These habits can strengthen your faith, improve your health, and give you a sense of stability. Remember: the little things you do each day add up to the big picture of your life. Keep taking small steps, and trust God to guide your journey forward.

CHAPTER 10

Building Strong Family Connections

Introduction
Family relationships can be both rewarding and challenging. Sometimes your family members are your closest friends, but you might also experience misunderstandings, arguments, or a sense of disconnection at home. As a Christian teen girl, you are called to love and respect your family, but real life can make this complicated.

In this chapter, we will explore practical ways to develop healthier connections with your parents, siblings, and other relatives. You will learn about communicating with respect, managing conflicts, and showing genuine care. These skills are important for a peaceful home and can help shape you into a compassionate person who treats others well. By applying biblical principles, you can brighten your household's atmosphere and strengthen the bonds that tie you together.

---

1. Why Family Matters

God created the family as a place where love, training, and support can grow. Even if your home situation has problems, there is an opportunity to learn about patience, forgiveness, and unity.

- **Foundation of Support**: In many cases, families offer a safety net. They know you well and can comfort you in tough times.
- **Spiritual Growth**: A Christian home can be a place where you pray together, serve together, and learn about God.
- **Life Lessons**: You practice negotiation, problem-solving, and empathy with your family members. These lessons can carry over into school, friendships, and future jobs.

Rarely Acknowledged Point: Even if your family is not "perfect," the shared history and experiences can create a deep sense of belonging. Choosing to invest in these relationships can yield strong emotional bonds.

2. Understanding Different Family Dynamics

Families come in all shapes and sizes. You might live with both parents, a single parent, grandparents, foster parents, or some other arrangement. Each family has its own patterns of behavior and communication.

- **Two-Parent Household**: Even with two parents, issues like work stress, sibling rivalries, or financial strains can cause tension.
- **Single-Parent Home**: One parent might carry many responsibilities. You might feel the need to help out more, which can be both rewarding and tiring.
- **Blended Families**: Step-parents or step-siblings can introduce changes in roles and routines. Adjusting can take patience.
- **Extended Family**: Some cultures value living with or near grandparents, uncles, and aunts. This can add more voices to daily life and decisions.

Encouragement: There is no one-size-fits-all family structure. Regardless of how your family is set up, you can practice kindness, patience, and respect.

---

3. Honoring Parents While Being Honest

Exodus 20:12 tells children to honor their father and mother, which can be confusing if you disagree with them or feel misunderstood. Honoring them does not mean you cannot share your thoughts, but it affects how you share them.

- **Speak Respectfully**: Use a calm tone and polite words when expressing disagreements. Avoid yelling or name-calling.
- **Listen Actively**: Give your parent the chance to explain their perspective. Even if you do not agree, understanding their reasoning shows maturity.
- **Choose the Right Time**: Avoid serious discussions when everyone is stressed or in a hurry. Look for a peaceful moment to bring up concerns.
- **Stay Truthful**: Honoring parents does not mean hiding important facts or lying. Be honest, but do it graciously.

Practical Example: If you feel your curfew is too early, approach your parent calmly. Say, "I understand you worry about my safety, but could we talk about adjusting my curfew by 30 minutes?" This respectful approach can lead to a more open dialogue.

4. Growing Closer to Siblings

Siblings can be your best friends or your greatest annoyance—sometimes on the same day! Learning to get along with them has lifelong benefits.

- **Set Boundaries**: If you share a room, talk about personal space and noise levels. Respect each other's belongings.
- **Encourage Each Other**: If you see your sibling doing well, let them know you are proud. This creates a positive vibe instead of competition.
- **Resolve Conflicts Quickly**: Small arguments can turn into big fights if left alone. Talk it out, apologize when wrong, and forgive.
- **Spend Quality Time**: Find an activity you both enjoy—like cooking, a board game, or a sport. Shared hobbies can deepen your bond.

Rarely Discussed Tip: You can pray for your siblings regularly. This not only helps them but also softens your heart toward them, making you less likely to hold grudges.

5. Handling Family Conflicts in a Godly Way

Every family has disagreements. The key is to handle them in a way that aligns with Christian values, rather than letting anger or pride get the best of you.

- **Stay Calm**: Proverbs 15:1 says a gentle answer turns away anger. Speak softly even if you are upset.
- **Focus on the Issue, Not the Person**: Instead of accusing a family member, address the action or problem. Say, "I felt hurt when you did X," rather than "You're always rude."
- **Seek a Win-Win**: Look for a solution that meets everyone's needs, if possible. This might involve compromise.
- **Forgive Each Other**: Holding onto bitterness can divide a family. Even if you cannot agree on everything, choose to release resentment.

Deep Thought: Conflict can be a chance to practice skills like patience, empathy, and mercy. Each resolved conflict strengthens the family if handled well.

6. Setting Healthy Boundaries with Relatives

Some family members might be overly critical, controlling, or even unsafe. While you are called to love them, it is important to set boundaries that protect your well-being.

- **Define Your Limits**: If a relative constantly insults your beliefs, you might limit how often you discuss faith with them.
- **Seek Adult Help if Necessary**: If you feel unsafe with any family member, tell a trusted adult, counselor, or church leader. Keeping silent can allow harm to continue.
- **Stay Respectful**: Setting boundaries does not mean being rude. You can stand firm without being hostile.
- **Know When to Leave the Conversation**: If things escalate, politely say you will continue talking later. Sometimes a break helps people calm down.

Note: God values your safety and emotional health. Boundaries are not selfish; they can be a form of wise stewardship of your life and mental well-being.

7. Family Bonding Activities

Creating positive family memories reduces tension and fosters understanding. These activities do not have to be expensive or complicated.

- **Family Meal Times**: Aim to eat together at least a few times a week. During the meal, ask about each other's day.
- **Shared Hobbies**: If your dad likes gardening, join him occasionally. If your mom enjoys puzzles, sit down and do one with her.
- **Outdoor Fun**: Go on a hike, have a picnic, or visit a local park. Being outside can put people in a calmer mood.
- **Volunteer Together**: Serving at a local shelter or participating in a church outreach can unite the family around a common cause.

Unique Tip: If you have younger siblings, reading them Bible stories or playing simple games can form happy memories for them and strengthen your bond.

8. Showing Love in Practical Ways

Love is more than a feeling. It involves actions that show care. Even small gestures can speak volumes to your family members.

- **Help Out**: Do a chore without being asked. Offer to watch a younger sibling so your parent can have a break.
- **Give Encouragement**: Write a short note or send a text telling a family member you appreciate them.
- **Recognize Milestones** : Recognize birthdays, academic achievements, or personal victories with a simple family moment.
- **Pray for Them**: Take a moment every day to lift up your family members in prayer. Ask God to bless them, guide them, and protect them.

Little-Known Fact: Many people have a "love language," a special way they feel most cared for (like words of affirmation, acts of service, or quality time). Noticing what makes your family feel loved can strengthen bonds.

---

9. Communicating with Clarity

Good communication is key to preventing misunderstandings. If you often say things like "You never listen" or "Whatever," it might shut down real conversation. Instead, try this:

- **Use "I" Statements**: "I feel stressed when the house is messy" is better than "You're so messy."
- **Listen Without Interrupting**: Give the speaker your full attention, repeat back what they said to confirm you heard it right, then respond.
- **Speak the Truth in Love**: Ephesians 4:15 tells us to speak truth lovingly. That means you do not hide the truth, but you deliver it kindly.
- **Ask Questions**: If you are not sure what your parent or sibling means, gently ask for clarification. This shows you care about their viewpoint.

Practical Example: If your mom seems worried, instead of brushing her off, you could ask, "Mom, you seem concerned. Can you tell me more about what's bothering you?" This can open the door to genuine conversation.

10. When You Disagree About Faith

Sometimes, you might be the only Christian in your home. Or perhaps you disagree with a family member on certain biblical interpretations. This can be sensitive.

- **Stay Respectful**: Do not belittle their beliefs or force yours on them.
- **Live Out Your Faith**: Often, consistent kindness and moral behavior speak louder than arguments. Let them see the fruit of your faith in how you treat them.
- **Pray for Opportunities**: Ask God to give you natural chances to talk about spiritual matters. Rushing it might push them away.
- **Seek Support**: A youth leader or a mentor can guide you on how to share faith gently at home.

Hopeful Reminder: God can use your quiet testimony to touch their hearts, even if it takes time. Be patient and keep praying.

---

11. Balancing Family Time and Independence

As a teenager, you want some freedom to explore your interests and develop your own identity. Your parents, meanwhile, might worry about letting you go. Finding balance requires wisdom:

- **Negotiate Privileges**: Show responsibility with the freedom you already have. If you handle it well, ask for a bit more independence.
- **Keep Parents Informed**: Telling your parents where you are going, who you are with, and when you will return builds trust.
- **Respect Their Rules**: Even if you think a rule is strict, try to follow it. Discuss calmly if you believe a rule is unfair, but avoid sneaking around or lying.
- **Set Boundaries for Yourself**: Sometimes, you need to pull back from social activities to fulfill family obligations or personal responsibilities. This shows maturity and earns your parents' confidence.

Seldom Mentioned Benefit: Showing respect for family guidelines often results in parents granting more freedom. They feel safer giving you space because you have shown you can handle it.

12. Supporting Parents in Their Stress

Parents are not superheroes, even though they often seem like they are juggling countless tasks. They have worries, work responsibilities, and personal issues. You can be a supportive presence rather than an extra source of stress.

- **Offer to Help**: Ask if there is anything you can do to lighten their load, like folding laundry or preparing a simple meal.
- **Give Them Space**: Sometimes, a parent might need a few minutes to unwind after work before diving into household duties.
- **Show Appreciation**: Thank them for things they often do for you—driving you to school, paying bills, or cooking meals.
- **Pray for Them**: Bring your parents' needs to God, whether it is their job stress or health concerns.

Advanced Thought: Seeing your parents as fellow human beings, not just authority figures, can shift your attitude. Recognizing their struggles can spark empathy and lead to more peaceful interactions.

---

13. Handling Serious Family Problems

Not all family challenges are minor. Issues like addiction, abuse, or ongoing conflicts can feel overwhelming and might require extra help.

- **Seek Help Early**: Talk to a trusted adult—a teacher, counselor, youth pastor—about what is happening. Keeping it hidden can make the problem worse.
- **Use Outside Resources**: If there is abuse or substance misuse, professional intervention might be needed. This could include therapy, support groups, or social services.
- **Rely on Prayer and Scripture**: The Bible reminds us that God is near the brokenhearted (Psalm 34:18). Cling to His promises, but also take practical steps to address the issue.
- **Stay Connected with Support**: Keep close to friends, church members, or mentors who can encourage you. Isolation can increase fear and despair.

Important Note: You are not betraying your family by seeking help. If the situation is harming you or others, getting help is an act of courage and can be the first step toward healing.

14. Building Shared Faith Routines

If your family is open to faith-based practices, you can strengthen connections through shared spiritual activities.

- **Family Devotion Time**: This could be once a week where you read a short Bible passage and discuss it together.
- **Group Prayer**: Praying together before meals or at bedtime can become a comforting routine.
- **Serving in Ministry**: If your family goes to the same church, volunteer together. Helping with a children's program or a charity drive creates a sense of teamwork.
- **Encourage One Another**: Share what God taught you in your personal devotions. Ask others if they have prayer requests.

Rare Benefit: When a family prays and worships together, it can defuse tensions. Spiritual unity often fosters deeper respect and understanding among household members.

---

15. Dealing with Sibling Rivalry

Rivalry can show up in many ways—competing for attention, jealous feelings over achievements, or constant teasing. While some competition can be normal, it should not lead to hatred or a lack of affection.

- **Recognize Everyone's Strengths**: Each sibling has unique talents. Compliment them sincerely and avoid comparing yourself.
- **Be Fair**: If you borrow a sibling's items, return them in good shape or with a thank you note. Show that you value their property and feelings.
- **Seek Common Ground**: If you both like music, share playlists. If you both like sports, practice together. Focusing on shared interests can reduce rivalry.
- **Celebrate Their Wins**: When your sibling achieves something, show genuine happiness for them.

Deep Insight: Overcoming sibling rivalry now can lead to a solid friendship in adulthood. Many adults regret the fights they had as teens and wish they had built stronger bonds earlier.

16. Technology Boundaries at Home

We live in a digital age, and devices can pull family members apart if not managed wisely. You might be in the same room but each glued to a screen.

- **Set Device-Free Times**: Decide as a family to avoid phones and tablets during meals or a designated hour in the evening.
- **Create Tech Zones**: Keep devices out of bedrooms at night, if possible. This helps everyone rest better and talk more face-to-face.
- **Use Shared Media**: Sometimes, watching a family-friendly show together or playing a multiplayer game can be a bonding experience, as long as it does not become a constant habit.
- **Be an Example**: If you want your siblings or parents to step away from screens, start by reducing your own usage. Show that you value real interaction.

Lesser-Known Fact: Studies show that households with regular device-free times often have better communication and deeper emotional connections.

17. Learning to Apologize and Forgive

No family is perfect. You will make mistakes, say things you regret, or let people down. Knowing how to apologize well and forgive swiftly is a powerful tool for peace.

- **Apologize Specifically**: Say what you are sorry for without making excuses. "I'm sorry for yelling at you yesterday. It was wrong, and I should have handled my stress better."
- **Avoid Shallow Excuses**: True apology admits fault and commits to change.
- **Accept Others' Apologies**: Even if you are still upset, acknowledge their effort to make things right. Healing often starts with a genuine acceptance of their remorse.
- **Learn to Let Go**: Holding grudges builds a wall between you. Forgiveness does not mean forgetting the offense, but releasing the anger that keeps you bound.

Practical Tip: Sometimes, writing an apology in a letter can help organize your thoughts. Then you can read it or hand it to the family member. This can reduce the chance of you losing track or getting too emotional mid-conversation.

18. Praying for Family Unity

When disagreements arise, or you feel distance growing, prayer can bring harmony.

- **Consistent Prayer**: Pray daily for each family member by name. Mention specific challenges or needs they have.
- **Group Prayer Requests**: Ask your parents or siblings how you can pray for them. This shows care and can break walls of tension.
- **Thank God for Them**: Even if you are mad at someone, thanking God for their positive traits can shift your heart.
- **Seek God's Guidance in Conflict**: Before a hard conversation, pray for wisdom and a loving attitude.

Deeper Note: Scripture says in Matthew 18:19-20 that when two agree in prayer, God is in their midst. Even praying with one sibling or parent can start a chain reaction of peace and understanding.

19. Looking Toward the Future

Your life with family might change as you get older—finishing high school, going to college, or moving out. Building a strong connection now can help maintain closeness despite future changes in living arrangements.

- **Plan Special Moments**: Time passes quickly. Make the most of the remaining years at home by creating positive memories and traditions.
- **Keep Communication Alive**: When you do move away, call or text your parents and siblings often. Show them you still care.
- **Respect Their Advice**: Even as you grow more independent, your family's guidance can still be valuable.
- **Offer Your Help**: When you visit, ask if you can assist with chores or errands. Show that you remain part of the family team.

Encouraging Thought: Healthy family ties can provide a consistent support system throughout adulthood. By investing in relationships now, you lay a solid foundation for future connections.

20. Moving Forward in Love and Respect

Building strong family connections takes time, patience, and prayer. Conflicts happen, but with the right tools and attitudes, you can grow closer to the people you call family. Your efforts can transform the tone of your household, bringing more peace, warmth, and unity. As you apply biblical principles and practical communication skills, you honor God and show that your faith impacts every area of life—including home.

Questions for Reflection

1. What is one way you can show respect to a parent or guardian this week?
2. Which small action could you do for a sibling to show kindness or support?
3. Are there any serious family issues you need to talk to a trusted adult about?

Practical Action Point
Pick one family member—maybe a sibling you do not get along with or a parent you have been arguing with—and do something kind for them. It could be helping with their chores, writing a sincere note of appreciation, or just spending quality time listening to them. Notice how this action affects your home's atmosphere.

Conclusion to Chapter 10
God designed families to be places of growth, love, and support. Even when your family has flaws or conflicts, you can help strengthen those bonds. Show respect, communicate openly, resolve conflicts with patience, and serve your family in practical ways. Through prayer and persistence, you can be a source of peace and unity in your home. As you move forward, you will see that the energy you put into family relationships not only improves life now but also sets a pattern for how you will treat people in the future.

CHAPTER 11

Staying Pure in Heart and Mind

Introduction
In a world filled with constant images, messages, and pressures, purity of heart and mind can seem hard to maintain. For a Christian teen girl, the call to purity is not only about physical boundaries, but also about thoughts, attitudes, and motivations. Even if you manage your outward actions, hidden thoughts can still distract you from living in a God-honoring way. How do you stay focused on good and right things in a society that seems to encourage the opposite?

In this chapter, we will look at the concept of staying pure in heart and mind in practical ways. You will learn tips to guard your thoughts, build healthy relationships, and avoid pitfalls that could harm your spiritual life. We will also connect these ideas to biblical truths, showing that purity is not just a set of rules, but an invitation to live in the light of God's goodness.

---

1. What Purity Really Means

When people hear the word "purity," they often think only of physical boundaries in dating. But purity is much broader. It includes what you think, what you watch or read, and what attitudes you allow in your heart.

- **Attitude of Respect and Honor**: A pure heart wants to honor God and others. You treat yourself and those around you with kindness, whether or not you like them.
- **Guarding Your Mind**: Being careful about the images, words, and ideas you allow into your thoughts. If certain songs or movies make you think harsh or unhealthy things, it might be wise to step away.
- **Speaking Truth**: Purity also covers truthfulness. Lying or being deceitful can pollute your heart just as much as impure images can.

Hidden Thought: Even if you do not break certain boundaries outwardly, you can still hold unhealthy fantasies, envy, or anger inside. True purity reaches your innermost desires and aims to make them clean.

2. Why the Heart and Mind Matter

The Bible often speaks about the heart being the wellspring of life (Proverbs 4:23). This means what you allow inside can shape how you act and who you become. If your heart is filled with goodness, your actions will reflect that goodness. If it is filled with jealousy or greed, that will show in your behavior.

- **Thoughts Lead to Actions**: Almost everything you do starts as a thought. If you repeatedly imagine something unhealthy, you might start moving toward it.
- **Protecting Your Emotions**: When you guard your mind, you also protect your emotions from confusion, shame, or unnecessary stress.
- **Honoring God**: God sees your inner life. Purity is not just about how others see you, but how you live before God.

Extra Insight: Many people believe they can "think whatever they want" as long as they do not do anything wrong outwardly. But thoughts can build strongholds that affect your future choices. Cleaning up your thought life is crucial.

---

3. Influences That Can Pollute Your Mind

Your mind is shaped by what you watch, read, and hear. Many media sources today promote ideas that do not line up with godly values.

- **Social Media**: Endless scrolling can expose you to images and messages that stir up envy, discontent, or lust.
- **Movies and TV Shows**: Some shows normalize rude behavior, gossip, or casual intimacy in ways that can slowly shift your moral boundaries.
- **Music**: Certain lyrics might glorify violence or sexual content. Listening repeatedly can dull your sense of right and wrong.
- **Peer Pressure**: Friends might share memes, jokes, or conversations that lead you to think about impure or harmful topics.

Practical Idea: Perform a quick media check on your phone or computer. Look at what you follow. If you find certain accounts or types of content that consistently push you toward harmful thoughts, consider muting or unfollowing them. It is a simple act that can create a big shift.

4. Setting Boundaries for Purity

Boundaries are like fences that protect what is valuable. When it comes to purity, boundaries are not about limiting your happiness, but about protecting you from regret and emotional pain.

- **Physical Boundaries**: If you are dating or thinking about relationships, discuss clear limits with a trusted mentor or parent. Decide how you will show affection without crossing lines you later regret.
- **Mental Boundaries**: This includes deciding which websites, apps, or shows are off-limits because they promote content that conflicts with biblical values.
- **Emotional Boundaries**: Sometimes, you can become emotionally attached in ways that cloud your judgment. Learn to keep a healthy pace in friendships or dating relationships so you do not give your heart away too quickly.
- **Accountability**: Find a trustworthy friend or mentor who will ask you the right questions. Knowing someone might check on your media habits or your thought life can strengthen your resolve.

Note: Boundaries are most effective if you decide on them before you are in a tempting situation. If you wait until you are already in the moment, it is easier to be swept away by emotions.

5. Tips for Guarding Your Thought Life

Changing your thought patterns is not something that happens overnight. It is an ongoing process, but there are daily steps you can take:

1. **Renew Your Mind with Scripture**: Read or listen to the Bible daily. Passages like Philippians 4:8 guide you to focus on what is pure and praiseworthy.
2. **Pray Throughout the Day**: When a negative or impure thought appears, say a quick prayer asking God to help you let it go and replace it with something righteous.

3. **Use Positive Inputs**: Surround yourself with uplifting music, encouraging books, or wholesome videos.
4. **Replace Bad Thoughts**: If you catch your mind drifting to a harmful scenario, immediately switch to a prepared positive thought or verse.
5. **Memorize Key Verses**: Having God's Word stored in your mind helps you fight unhealthy thoughts from the inside out.

Deeper Technique: Some people keep a short list of "thought replacements" on their phone—positive statements or verses they read whenever they notice their mind going off track.

---

6. Overcoming Temptations

Temptation is normal and happens to everyone, but how you respond is what matters. For instance, you might feel drawn to look up certain online content you know is not good, or you might be tempted to dwell on a daydream that leads your heart away from good things.

- **Stay Away from Triggers**: If you know a certain time of day or place sparks negative thoughts, change your routine. Avoid being alone in situations where you can easily access harmful content.
- **Have a Plan**: Decide in advance what you will do when tempted—perhaps sending a quick text to a trusted friend or stepping outside for fresh air.
- **Remember God's Help**: 1 Corinthians 10:13 reminds us that God provides a way to escape temptation if we look for it.
- **View Mistakes as Warnings**: If you slip up, do not wallow in shame. Instead, see it as a warning sign that you need stronger boundaries or better accountability.

Key Point: Temptation itself is not a sin. It is about what you do next. Quickly turn to God, not away, and He can help you stand strong.

---

7. Seeking Forgiveness and Grace

No one is perfect. You might have made mistakes that make you feel "too far gone" or unworthy of a pure life. Yet the core message of Christianity is that God forgives and restores those who come to Him.

- **Confession**: Talk to God openly about your failures. Holding them in only increases guilt.
- **Believe in Cleansing**: 1 John 1:9 says that if we confess our sins, God is faithful to forgive and purify us.
- **Break the Cycle of Shame**: Guilt can lead you to hide from God or fall deeper into harmful habits. Recognize that God wants to lift you up, not condemn you.
- **Start Fresh**: Every day is a new chance to live according to God's grace. Even if you stumbled yesterday, you can move forward today with hope.

Encouraging Thought: King David in the Bible committed serious sins but sincerely repented. His writings in the Psalms show that God's mercy can mend a broken heart and bring it back to purity.

---

8. Navigating Friendships and Peer Pressure

Your friends have a big influence on your decisions. If they encourage gossip, crude jokes, or unhealthy relationships, it may be harder to keep your heart and mind pure.

- **Be Selective**: Choose friends who respect your choices. People who mock your desire to stay pure are not truly supportive.
- **Stand Up for Values**: When peers push you to watch or do something you feel is wrong, calmly say you are not comfortable. You do not need to lecture them, but stand firm.
- **Offer Alternatives**: Suggest activities that are fun yet healthy. If your group usually watches edgy shows, propose a lighthearted movie or a board game night.
- **Seek Mentors**: Connect with older girls or women in your church who have walked this road. Their advice can keep you motivated.

Rare Tip: If you feel outnumbered by negative influences, look for a Christian youth group or club. There you might find peers who share your commitment to a clean mind and heart.

9. Body Image and Purity

Purity also includes how you view your body and other people's bodies. In a world that often objectifies people, it is easy to start seeing yourself or others in a shallow way.

- **Respect Your Body**: Treat it as a valuable creation of God. That means not putting it on display to gain attention, but also not disliking it because it is not "perfect."
- **Avoid Comparing**: Constantly thinking, "I wish I had her figure" or "I'm better looking than her" can lead to pride or insecurity—both can poison your heart.
- **Dress Wisely**: Modesty does not mean hiding who you are, but choosing clothing that does not provoke harmful thoughts in yourself or others.
- **Speak Kindly About Yourself**: Negative self-talk or jokes about your appearance can hurt your heart. Remember, your worth is in who God made you to be, not in matching society's trends.

Practical Exercise: When you catch yourself criticizing your body in the mirror, pause and say a short prayer thanking God for your health and the functions your body can do. This trains your mind to value what is real rather than chasing unattainable ideals.

---

10. Dating with a Pure Mindset

If you enter the dating scene as a teen, purity in relationships is a topic you cannot ignore. It is not just about physical boundaries, but also emotional and spiritual health.

- **Know Your Standards**: Sit down (maybe with a parent or mentor) and outline what you believe is acceptable in a dating relationship, from physical contact to how much time you spend alone.
- **Pray Together (If Both Are Believers)**: Including God in your relationship is a strong way to keep focused on purity and respect.
- **Avoid Compromising Situations**: Spending time alone late at night, or browsing questionable online spaces together can lower your guard.

- **Stay Honest with Emotions**: If you realize you are becoming too attached or crossing boundaries, address it immediately. Seeking counsel early can prevent deeper hurt.

Reminder: Your value does not come from having a partner. If you sense that dating is too big a responsibility for you right now, waiting is a mature decision.

---

11. Dealing with Media Curiosity

Many teens are curious about mature or explicit content. They might turn to the internet to see "what it's all about." But this curiosity can trap you in a cycle of unhealthy thoughts.

- **Recognize Curiosity**: It is normal to wonder. However, ask yourself if the material you are seeking will truly help you learn in a healthy way, or if it is simply fueling lust or confusion.
- **Choose Educational Resources Wisely**: If you have questions about sexuality or relationships, a trusted adult or a Christian resource can provide clarity without polluting your mind.
- **Use Filters**: Install software that blocks explicit sites. This reduces the chance of stumbling on harmful images.
- **Have Open Conversations**: Talking with a parent, older sibling, or mentor about these topics can feel awkward, but it might prevent secretive exploration that leads to guilt or addiction.

Little-Known Fact: Many surveys suggest that early exposure to explicit materials can distort a person's view of real relationships and intimacy, leading to issues in trust and self-esteem later on.

---

12. Handling Shame and Regret

Maybe you have already viewed things you regret or had experiences that left you feeling unclean. Shame can make you feel stuck, but God offers a way out.

- **Bring It to Light**: Shame thrives in the dark. Confide in a mentor or a Christian counselor. Let them help you walk through healing.

- **God's Redemption**: Scripture is filled with examples of people who messed up and were restored by God's love. He can do the same for you.
- **Work Through Emotions**: You might feel sadness, anger, or confusion about what happened. That is normal. Talk with someone who can guide you toward forgiveness (for yourself or others).
- **Forgive Yourself**: Holding onto regret does not make you holier. It only keeps you trapped. Accept the grace God gives and move forward with wisdom.

Encouragement: The cross of Christ reminds us that no sin is too great for God to forgive. Your story can continue in freedom rather than remain in past mistakes.

---

13. Building a Supportive Circle

Trying to live with purity in heart and mind on your own can be very challenging. A community of supportive friends and mentors can keep you accountable and encourage you.

- **Join Church Activities**: Being involved in youth groups, Bible studies, or church events helps you meet people who share your values.
- **Form a Small Group**: Even having one or two friends committed to honesty and purity can be enough to keep each other motivated.
- **Pray for One Another**: Knowing someone is praying for your thoughts and decisions can give you strength when you are tempted.
- **Learn from Role Models**: Talk to older believers about how they handled temptations. Their stories might guide you away from pitfalls.

Rare Advantage: Strong friendships built on shared faith often grow deeper because you are helping each other stay aligned with the truths you believe in. This bond can outlast superficial connections based on looks or popular trends.

---

14. Gratitude as a Tool for Purity

Being thankful can guard your heart from negative emotions and temptations. When you practice gratitude, you focus on what God has blessed you with instead of longing for what is wrong or harmful.

- **Daily Thank-You List**: Each morning or evening, write down three things you are thankful for. This simple habit refocuses your mind on the good.
- **Thanking God Out Loud**: When you feel stressed, pause and say something like, "God, I thank You for my family, for my meal today, and for getting me through school."
- **Shifting Perspective**: Gratitude can also protect against jealousy or lust. When you appreciate what you have, you are less likely to crave what you should not have.

Surprising Benefit: Studies show that people who practice gratitude regularly are often less anxious and more content, which indirectly supports staying pure in thoughts, because a content mind is less prone to harmful fixations.

---

15. Being a Light to Others

Choosing purity is not only about your personal well-being. It is also a testimony to those around you. When classmates or friends notice you do not laugh at certain jokes or watch certain shows, they might become curious about your reason.

- **Gentle Explanation**: If they ask, explain calmly that you want to keep your heart and mind clean because of your faith and personal values.
- **Avoid Self-Righteousness**: Share your stance humbly, not looking down on them. Emphasize that it is a choice you made to honor God and protect your mind.
- **Guide Younger Girls**: If you have younger siblings or girls who look up to you at church, show them that purity is possible and fulfilling, not dull or stuffy.
- **Respond with Kindness**: You might face teasing or misunderstanding. Keep your cool and continue to show kindness. Your steady example can plant seeds of respect.

Perspective: You never know who might be struggling internally, hoping for a way to live a cleaner life. Your example might be the sign they need.

16. Checking Your Inner Motivations

Staying pure in heart and mind is not about pretending to be perfect. Sometimes you can avoid certain behaviors but still be motivated by fear of judgment or a desire to look good in front of others. True purity involves the right motives.

- **Serve God, Not Image**: Ask yourself if you are making these choices to glorify God or just to appear "holy." Authentic purity aims to please God, not boost your reputation.
- **Confess Pride**: If you find yourself bragging about your pure lifestyle, that can be a sign of pride creeping in.
- **Guard Against Legalism**: Following strict rules without love or faith can lead to harsh judgment of others. Remember that Jesus always combined truth with compassion.
- **Focus on Love**: Jesus said the greatest commands are to love God and love others (Matthew 22:37-39). Purity should flow from this heart of love.

Deep Reflection: Sometimes a quick self-check question helps: "Am I doing this because I love God and want to honor Him, or just to keep a good image?" Answer honestly and adjust your heart as needed.

---

17. Continuous Growth in Purity

Purity is not a one-time choice; it is a lifestyle that grows as you mature. Over time, the challenges you face might change, but the principles remain the same.

- **Regular Self-Evaluation**: From time to time, ask yourself if your thoughts, media choices, or friendships are still healthy. If you spot a slip, correct course quickly.
- **Welcome God's Discipline**: If God points out an area of impurity in your life, do not ignore it. Take steps to fix it through prayer, repentance, or seeking guidance.
- **Stay Teachable**: Listen to sermons, read Christian articles, and talk with mature believers to keep learning about what purity looks like in different seasons of life.
- **Find Joy in Obedience**: Purity should not feel like a grim duty. The more you align with God's ways, the more peace and joy you often experience.

Insight: Some teens mistakenly think that once they have made a choice for purity, they can relax. But the world constantly bombards you with new temptations. Staying alert and connected to God is a lifelong process.

---

18. Trusting God's Plan for Your Life

Impure thoughts often spring from discontent or a need for thrills. You might feel that you are missing out on the "fun" that others boast about. In such moments, trusting God's plan is critical.

- **God's Goodness**: Believe that God is not withholding joy from you. He designed boundaries to protect you, not to make your life dull.
- **Future Blessings**: If you keep your mind and heart guarded now, you can enjoy healthier relationships in the future, free from guilt or haunting memories.
- **Patience**: Some desires are natural but need the right context (like sexual desires within marriage). Trust that God knows the right timing.
- **Purpose**: When you stick to God's path, your sense of purpose and identity grows stronger, reducing the urge to seek false excitement.

Thought to Remember: God sees the bigger picture. If you remain faithful in small decisions today, you set yourself up for bigger blessings and deeper spiritual growth tomorrow.

---

19. Practical Daily Checklist for Purity

Since purity can feel like a huge concept, here is a simple checklist you could adapt in your daily life:

1. **Morning Prayer**: Ask God to protect your thoughts and words throughout the day.
2. **Media Monitor**: Quickly review your phone or computer. Unfollow or mute anything that pushes you toward impure content.
3. **Accountability**: Send a short message to a trusted friend or mentor, letting them know your goal for the day (like avoiding certain sites or focusing on positive thoughts).

4. **Check-In with Scripture**: Read at least a short verse or passage. Let it remind you of truth.
5. **Evening Review**: Before bed, reflect on your day. Thank God for successes, and if you stumbled, confess it and make a plan to avoid a repeat.

Small Tip: Consistency is key. Even if it seems simple or repetitive, daily actions eventually form strong habits that keep your heart and mind on track.

---

20. Closing Thoughts and Next Steps

Staying pure in heart and mind is an ongoing commitment that will bless every area of your life—your friendships, your relationship with God, and your future goals. This pursuit does not guarantee a life free from struggle, but it does promise fewer regrets and a closer connection with God. By carefully choosing what you allow into your thoughts, setting wise boundaries, and leaning on God's grace when you fall, you can walk through your teen years with a clear conscience and steady spirit.

Questions for Reflection

1. Which area of purity do you find most challenging—thoughts, media, or friendships?
2. What is one boundary you can set this week to protect your mind and heart?
3. Who could serve as an accountability partner to encourage you in this commitment?

Practical Action Point
Choose one media source (social media account, app, show) that regularly leads you toward negative or impure thoughts. Mute or unfollow it for one week. Notice any changes in how you feel or what you think about. If you see a positive difference, consider making the change permanent or adjusting your boundaries more widely.

CHAPTER 12

Becoming a Leader at School and Church

Introduction
When people hear the word "leader," they might picture someone in charge of a large crowd or making speeches on a stage. But leadership can happen anywhere—even if you are a teen who thinks you are just "ordinary." God has a special purpose for everyone, and He can use you as a leader in your school, church, or community. Leadership does not always mean having a formal title; it can be as simple as influencing others in positive ways.

In this chapter, we will talk about what it means to be a Christian leader. We will cover traits like humility, responsibility, and courage. You will learn how to stand out without being bossy, how to guide others while still being respectful, and how to handle the responsibility that comes with leadership. Whether you want to start a club at school or help lead a small group at church, these lessons can help you develop into the kind of leader who honors God.

---

1. Rethinking Leadership

Many people assume a leader must be loud, have an outgoing personality, or be academically or athletically gifted. However, biblical examples show that leadership can come from anyone willing to trust God.

- **Moses**: He felt inadequate because of a speech problem, yet God used him to lead Israel out of slavery.
- **Esther**: A young woman who risked her life to speak to a king for the sake of her people.
- **Timothy**: A young church leader who needed encouragement not to let anyone look down on him for his youth (1 Timothy 4:12).

Lesson: Being a leader is more about character than about charm or external achievements. If you focus on godly traits like humility, kindness, and honesty, you can guide others in any setting.

---

2. The Heart of a Servant Leader

Jesus modeled servant leadership by washing His disciples' feet (John 13:1-17), showing that greatness in God's kingdom means putting others first.

- **Putting Others Before Yourself**: Be willing to do small tasks nobody else wants to do. This selflessness sets a powerful example.
- **Listening More Than Speaking**: A servant leader pays attention to others' ideas, struggles, and needs. When people feel heard, they trust you more.
- **Aiming for Team Success**: Instead of competing for personal recognition, a servant leader helps everyone do well.
- **Staying Humble**: Pride can destroy leadership. Regularly remind yourself that leadership is about serving, not dominating.

Rare Fact: People often assume leadership is about ordering people around. But many effective Christian leaders focus on service and genuine care, earning respect rather than demanding it.

---

3. Identifying Your Leadership Opportunities

You might not see yourself as a leader yet, but opportunities might be right under your nose:

- **School Clubs**: If you have a special interest—like art, science, or volunteering—you can start or join a club. Offer to organize events or help newcomers.
- **Class Projects**: Volunteer to coordinate group assignments. This can teach you planning and cooperation.
- **Church Ministries**: Youth choir, children's ministry, ushering, or tech support during services are ways to practice leadership skills.
- **Community Outreach**: Helping at a local charity or organizing a neighborhood cleanup can show you how to lead small teams for a good cause.

Tip: Do not wait for a fancy title like "president" or "head." Leadership can be as small as helping classmates stay focused during a group assignment or comforting a friend who is upset.

4. Developing Confidence Without Pride

Some teens struggle with feeling too shy to lead, while others might dive in with too much arrogance. True leadership balances confidence and humility.

- **Know Your Worth in God**: Confidence grows when you trust that you are valued by God. You do not need others' approval to validate you.
- **Admit Weaknesses**: When you are wrong or do not know an answer, say so. People respect honesty more than fake perfection.
- **Celebrate Others**: Point out others' strengths. This encourages teamwork and reduces selfish behavior.
- **Stay Open to Feedback**: Be willing to learn from teachers, mentors, or peers who correct you. Their advice can help you refine your leadership approach.

Golden Nugget: Insecurity can lead to pride if you compensate by showing off. True confidence stems from knowing God's truth about who you are and what you can do with His help.

---

5. Building Trust and Integrity

Leaders cannot function without trust. If people doubt your honesty or reliability, they will be reluctant to follow you.

- **Keep Your Word**: If you promise to bring snacks for a club meeting, bring them. If you say you will help someone study, follow through.
- **Be Consistent**: Aim to be the same person at church, at school, and at home. Integrity means not acting one way in public and another in private.
- **Confess Mistakes**: If you fail at a task or forget a commitment, own up to it. Apologize and make it right if you can.
- **Uphold Morals**: Even if it costs popularity points, do not lie, cheat, or gossip. Those choices can crack the foundation of trust.

Practical Example: If you are leading a youth group game night, show up prepared and on time. Let your words and actions match. Over time, people will trust you because they see your consistent honesty.

6. Communicating Effectively

Leaders need to share ideas, guide teams, and solve conflicts. Communication skills can be developed through practice and attention.

- **Active Listening**: Focus on the speaker, ask questions, and summarize what they said to ensure clarity.
- **Clear Directions**: When you assign tasks or share instructions, break them into steps. This helps everyone know what to do and reduces confusion.
- **Respectful Tone**: Even if you disagree with someone, avoid harsh words. Show empathy and talk about the issue, not the person.
- **Nonverbal Signals**: Make eye contact, stand with a straight posture, and speak at a calm pace. This makes you appear more confident and engaged.

Little-Known Secret: Many top leaders practice speaking in front of a mirror or with close friends to refine how they come across. You can do the same to notice any awkward habits or unclear phrases.

---

7. Handling Conflict Like a Leader

Conflict is inevitable in groups. Good leaders do not avoid disagreements; they handle them in a way that leads to growth and unity.

- **Address Issues Quickly**: Letting small resentments build can explode later. Speak up calmly when you see a problem.
- **Listen to All Sides**: Give each person a chance to explain their viewpoint. This shows fairness.
- **Focus on Solutions**: Shift from "Who caused this?" to "How can we fix it together?"
- **Stay Calm and Respectful**: Yelling or insults only make the conflict worse. Maintaining composure models good behavior for everyone else.

Unique Angle: Sometimes, as a young leader, you might feel unsure about stepping into conflict. But your willingness to mediate and seek peaceful resolutions can win you respect from peers and adults alike.

8. Balancing School Leadership and Faith

If you step into leadership roles at school, you might face moral dilemmas. For example, a club might plan an event that goes against your faith, or you might be pressured to compromise your beliefs to fit in.

- **Draw Clear Lines**: Know ahead of time what you will not support or do. Communicate these boundaries politely.
- **Offer Alternatives**: If an event conflicts with your values, suggest a different theme or approach that stays true to the group's goals while respecting your principles.
- **Be Ready for Reactions**: Some people might mock you. Others might admire your standing firm. Stay gracious, no matter the response.
- **Lean on Prayer**: Ask God for wisdom on how to lead without bending your faith. He can open doors for new ideas that bless everyone.

Reminder: You cannot control how others react to your beliefs, but you can control your attitude. Remember Daniel in the Bible, who kept his faith even under pressure, and ended up positively influencing a whole kingdom.

---

9. Leading in Church Activities

Church can be a great place to develop leadership skills because the environment often encourages growth, and you can find supportive mentors.

- **Volunteer for Roles**: Ask if you can help plan a youth event, participate in worship, or organize a charity drive.
- **Support Your Leaders**: Offer help to youth pastors, Sunday school teachers, or event coordinators. They might let you lead segments of a program or handle small groups.
- **Encourage Younger Kids**: If there are children's programs, stepping in as a helper teaches you responsibility and sets an example for little ones.
- **Stay Open to Guidance**: Church leaders can give you practical tips for teamwork, conflict resolution, and spiritual leadership.

Hidden Benefit: Leading in a church setting often deepens your personal relationship with God because you learn to rely on Him for direction, especially when planning faith-based events or dealing with spiritual questions.

10. Time Management for Busy Leaders

When you start taking on leadership tasks, your schedule can fill quickly. Balancing school, chores, personal life, and leadership is a real challenge.

- **Use a Planner**: Write down deadlines, meeting times, and personal responsibilities. Seeing them in one place helps you avoid double-booking.
- **Set Priorities**: Determine which tasks need your immediate attention and which can wait or be delegated.
- **Avoid Overcommitting**: It is better to do a few things well than to do many things poorly. Learn to say "no" when you are at capacity.
- **Schedule Rest**: Burnout can happen if you never relax. Plan small breaks or fun activities to recharge.

Advanced Tip: Some successful teen leaders use a simple technique called "time blocking." They dedicate certain hours to studying, certain hours to chores, and certain hours to leadership tasks. This keeps them organized and less stressed.

11. Dealing with Criticism and Failure

No leader is perfect. You might plan an event that flops or make a decision that upsets someone. Handling criticism well is part of growing in leadership.

- **Listen with an Open Mind**: Even if the tone is harsh, see if there is any valid feedback.
- **Apologize if Needed**: If you genuinely made a mistake, own it. Show you are willing to learn and improve.
- **Reject False Guilt**: If someone criticizes you just because they do not like your faith or your style, do not let it drag you down unnecessarily.
- **Learn and Move On**: Failure can be the best teacher. Evaluate what went wrong, fix it for next time, and let it go.

Encouraging Perspective: The Bible is full of leaders like Peter who failed at times (denying Jesus) but were later restored and used mightily. Failure is not the end; it can be a stepping stone to better leadership.

12. Leading Through Example

Actions speak louder than words. People watch what you do more than what you say. Leading by example means living out your values consistently.

- **Be Respectful**: If you demand respect but do not show it to others, they will see the double standard.
- **Work Hard**: If you slack off, others might do the same. Show diligence in schoolwork and responsibilities.
- **Keep a Good Attitude**: Negative gossip or complaining can spread quickly. If you stay positive and solution-focused, others may follow suit.
- **Follow Rules**: If you break school or church rules while leading, it undermines your authority. Model obedience to guidelines.

Subtle Hint: Even small acts—like picking up trash in the hallway, helping a teacher carry supplies, or saying kind words—can plant seeds of leadership in your environment.

13. Encouraging Diversity and Teamwork

Leaders who recognize each person's unique gifts can build stronger teams. You do not have to be the best at everything. Instead, find people who have talents you lack.

- **Identify Strengths**: Notice who is good at organizing, who is artistic, who communicates well, etc. Assign tasks that fit these skills.
- **Listen to Input**: Invite team members to share ideas. This fosters creativity and shared ownership of the project.
- **Be Fair and Inclusive**: Avoid showing favoritism. Make sure everyone has a chance to contribute.
- **Celebrate Group Success**: When the team meets a goal, acknowledge everyone's effort. This builds unity and motivation.

Rare Bonus: By highlighting diverse talents, you may discover gifts in people they never knew they had, boosting their confidence and loyalty to the team.

14. Keeping Your Spiritual Life Strong

As a Christian leader, your spiritual health matters more than your outward achievements. If you neglect your relationship with God, you risk burnout and confusion.

- **Regular Devotions**: Spend time in prayer and Scripture reading, even when busy. God's guidance can prevent mistakes and refuel you.
- **Seek Wise Counsel**: Talk to pastors or spiritual mentors about your leadership roles. Their insights can keep you grounded.
- **Stay Humble Before God**: Praise Him for successes and ask for help in your struggles. Dependence on God protects you from pride.
- **Fellowship with Other Believers**: Surrounding yourself with supportive Christians can keep you accountable in your leadership journey.

Thought: Jesus often withdrew to pray alone (Luke 5:16). If He needed that closeness with the Father, how much more do we need it?

15. Overcoming Fear and Anxiety

You might worry about public speaking, making the wrong call, or looking silly in front of classmates. These fears are normal, but they do not have to control you.

- **Prepare Thoroughly**: Knowing your material and practicing can reduce jitters.
- **Pray for Courage**: Ask God for a calm spirit and a reminder that you are serving Him, not just people's opinions.
- **Visualize Success**: Imagine yourself doing well, focusing on positive outcomes instead of failure.
- **Take It One Step at a Time**: You do not need to fix every problem at once. Deal with each challenge as it comes.

Inspiring Reality: Many famous Christian figures felt fear or insecurity, but God used them anyway. Stepping through fear can lead to growth and deeper faith.

16. Handling Peer Jealousy

Not everyone will be happy to see you lead. Some peers might envy your role or spread negativity. A good leader deals with this gracefully.

- **Show Kindness**: Return any coldness with respect and friendliness. Sometimes, their jealousy might fade when they see you are not hostile.
- **Do Not Boast**: Stay low-key about your achievements. Share credit with the team whenever possible.
- **Set Boundaries**: If someone's jealousy turns into bullying, seek help from a teacher, pastor, or mentor.
- **Pray for Them**: Jealousy often comes from personal insecurity. Asking God to heal their hurts can change the atmosphere.

Important Thought: You cannot force someone to like you, but you can control your response. Maintaining integrity often wins respect in the long run.

---

17. Mentoring Others

As you grow in leadership, you can pass on what you learn to younger teens or new group members. Mentoring someone else helps you refine your own skills and multiply positive impact.

- **Offer Guidance**: If a younger girl in your youth group is nervous about leading prayer, coach her through it.
- **Build Confidence**: Highlight her strengths and give constructive feedback to help her improve.
- **Set a Regular Check-In**: Have short chats weekly or monthly to see how she is doing.
- **Acknowledge Growth**: Let her know when you see improvement. Encourage her to keep stretching her abilities.

Hidden Reward: Mentoring creates a ripple effect, raising new leaders who can also pass on the lessons. Your efforts can bless multiple generations within a church or community.

18. Keeping a Long-Term Vision

True leadership does not just look at immediate results. It considers what will benefit people in the future, even if it requires patience or sacrifice.

- **Set Achievable Goals**: Break big dreams into smaller steps. Celebrate each step, then aim for the next.
- **Stay Focused on Values**: If a shortcut conflicts with honesty or kindness, do not take it. Long-term integrity is more important than short-term gain.
- **Encourage Sustainability**: If you start a project, train others to continue it after you graduate or move on.
- **Reflect Often**: Ask yourself, "How will this decision affect my group next month or next year?" This mindset helps you lead responsibly.

Advanced Perspective: Kingdom-minded leaders think about God's eternal purposes, not just short-lived popularity. This can alter how you choose projects or handle disputes.

---

19. Celebrating Wins and Learning from Losses

Leadership involves successes and failures. Marking achievements and extracting lessons from losses will shape you into a well-rounded leader.

- **Mark Achievements**: If your team hits a milestone, give credit to each member. Maybe plan a small get-together or group prayer of thanks.
- **Learn from Mistakes**: Instead of avoiding the topic, discuss what went wrong, how to prevent it next time, and what you learned about yourself or the team.
- **Keep Records**: Some leaders jot down lessons in a journal. Reviewing them later can keep you from repeating old errors.
- **Stay Grateful**: Whether in wins or losses, continue thanking God for the chance to lead and grow.

Rare Perspective: Great leaders often say they learned more from tough times than from easy successes. Embracing hardships can help you mature faster.

20. Moving Forward with a Leader's Heart

Leadership is not a destination but a process. As you practice serving, listening, guiding, and inspiring others, you grow step by step. Keep your heart humble, your mind open to learning, and your spirit connected to God. In school, you can show fairness and kindness; at church, you can be a role model of faithfulness. Over time, your efforts can influence people for good and show them a glimpse of Christ's love through your actions.

Questions for Reflection

1. What small leadership role could you take on right now at school or church?
2. How can you improve your communication skills to lead others more effectively?
3. Who is a strong Christian leader you admire, and what traits of theirs can you adopt?

Practical Action Point
Pick one leadership skill (like conflict resolution, active listening, or organizing tasks) and focus on improving it this week. For example, if you want to practice active listening, then in every conversation, do not interrupt and do your best to repeat back what the speaker said. Notice if it changes how people respond to you.

Conclusion to Chapter 12
Becoming a leader at school and church is about more than holding a title. It is about influencing others through service, humility, integrity, and faith. You can start in small ways—by showing kindness, solving problems, or guiding a group project. As you develop these skills and rely on God's help, you will discover that leadership is within your reach, no matter how ordinary you feel. Step by step, you can become a trusted voice and a steady light, helping others grow and follow God's path.

CHAPTER 13

Handling Doubts and Questions

Introduction
Having doubts and questions is a normal part of faith. Sometimes, you might feel sure about what you believe. Other times, you might wonder if God really listens or if certain Bible stories are true. You may be unsure how Christianity fits with what you learn at school or see in the news. These feelings can be confusing, but they do not mean your faith is weak. In fact, asking honest questions can help you grow.

In this chapter, we will talk about handling doubts in a healthy way. You will learn approaches to seek answers, talk with trusted people, and strengthen your faith. The goal is not to pretend you never wonder about anything. Instead, you will discover how to face your questions with courage and honesty, trusting that God can lead you to the truth.

---

1. Understanding the Nature of Doubt

Doubt is the feeling of uncertainty or a struggle to believe. It is not the same as having no faith. In fact, a person can have genuine trust in God while still wrestling with questions about details of the Bible, Christian living, or moral issues.

- **Examples in Scripture**: You are not alone. Some biblical figures also had questions. For example, Thomas wanted proof that Jesus rose from the dead (John 20:24-29). Even John the Baptist, who prepared the way for Jesus, sent disciples to ask if Jesus was really the Messiah (Matthew 11:2-3).
- **Healthy vs. Harmful Doubt**: Healthy doubt pushes you to learn more and refine your beliefs. Harmful doubt causes you to give up on seeking answers. The difference often lies in your willingness to keep searching.

Key Reminder: Doubt does not surprise God. He is not upset that you have questions. He wants you to seek Him with sincerity.

2. Common Sources of Doubt

Doubt can arise from many places. Identifying where it comes from can help you address it more effectively.

1. **Conflicting Messages**: You might hear one thing at church and another in science class or from friends. This can create confusion.
2. **Personal Pain**: A loss or traumatic event can cause you to question why a good God would allow suffering.
3. **Cultural Shifts**: Social media and pop culture may present values or lifestyles that seem to clash with Christian teaching.
4. **Unanswered Prayers**: When you pray for something important and do not see the result you want, it can lead to doubt about God's goodness or power.

Practical Tip: Make a note of the topics that spark questions in your mind—like the creation of the universe, miracles in the Bible, or the existence of suffering. Knowing your concern helps you find relevant resources to explore answers.

---

3. Approaches to Finding Answers

When questions arise, the best approach is to investigate them rather than ignore them. The more you learn, the better you can form a grounded faith.

- **Study the Bible Thoroughly**: Do not rely only on what you hear from others. Read the passages yourself. Use a study Bible or reputable commentary to gain context.
- **Ask Mentors**: Talk to a youth pastor, a parent who is strong in faith, or a knowledgeable teacher. Sharing your questions can lead to deeper discussions and insights.
- **Check Christian Apologetics**: "Apologetics" means reasoned arguments or writings in defense of the faith. Many authors address tough questions about God, the Bible, and ethics. They present logical and historical support for Christian beliefs.
- **Compare Various Perspectives**: It can be helpful to read how different theologians or churches interpret certain passages or issues. While this might present multiple views, it also shows how believers reason through the same questions.

Deeper Insight: Sometimes, people fear that digging into tough questions will weaken their faith. In reality, honest searching often makes your faith stronger and more personal because you understand why you believe, not just what you believe.

---

4. The Role of Prayer in Doubt

When doubt arises, prayer might feel awkward. But talking to God about your confusion can bring comfort and clarity.

- **Honest Conversation**: You can say, "God, I'm not sure about this aspect of my faith. Please help me see the truth." King David did something similar in the Psalms, openly sharing his complaints and worries with the Lord.
- **Listening to God's Guidance**: After you pray, be attentive. You may find a verse that seems to address your concern or a wise friend who brings helpful insight. Sometimes, you get an inner sense of peace about a matter.
- **Waiting Patiently**: Answers may not come instantly. Prayer is about trust as much as it is about receiving immediate solutions. Keep a journal of your prayers and look back later to see if certain doubts have resolved over time.

Key Thought: Prayer is not just for making requests. It is also for building a relationship with God, even in times of uncertainty. This relationship can anchor you when you do not have all the answers.

---

5. Talking to Trusted People

Trying to handle all your doubts alone can feel overwhelming. Reaching out to others who care about you and your spiritual journey can lighten the burden.

- **Choosing the Right People**: Look for individuals who are both understanding and knowledgeable in Christian matters. This might include your pastor, a small group leader, a faithful family member, or a counselor who shares your beliefs.

- **Being Open**: Explain your questions clearly. For instance, say something like, "I struggle with why God allows natural disasters," or "I'm not sure how science and Genesis fit together." This specificity helps them address your actual concerns.
- **Being Willing to Listen**: You might hear answers you do not like or that take time to accept. Keep an open mind and consider what they say before rejecting it.
- **Maintaining Respect**: Even if you do not agree with everything they share, show gratitude for their time and perspective. This attitude keeps the conversation warm and productive.

Practical Example: You could set up a monthly chat with a mentor or join a Bible study group that welcomes questions. Regular discussions create a safe space to raise doubts as they come up.

---

6. Reconciling Faith and Science

One area that often sparks doubts is the relationship between Christianity and science. You might wonder if believing in the Bible means rejecting scientific discoveries.

- **Understanding Their Roles**: Science explores how the natural world works, while faith speaks to questions of meaning, purpose, and morality. They address different aspects of reality.
- **Seeking Christian Scientists**: Many respected scientists are Christians who see no conflict between their research and their faith. Learning about their perspectives can be reassuring.
- **Avoiding False Choices**: Some say you have to pick between faith and facts. That can be a false choice. While some biblical interpretations might clash with certain scientific theories, other interpretations might align well.
- **Recognizing the Bible's Purpose**: Scripture does not always present itself as a science textbook. It uses stories, poetry, and teachings to convey spiritual truths, salvation history, and moral principles. That does not remove its authority, but it helps us respect the context in which it was written.

Encouraging Thought: God created the universe and gave us the curiosity to explore it. Honest science can lead to a greater appreciation of God's creativity and wisdom, rather than forcing us away from faith.

7. Addressing Suffering and Evil

One of the toughest doubts is why a good God would allow pain, injustice, and tragedy. This question has challenged believers for centuries.

- **Biblical Insights**: The Bible acknowledges the reality of suffering. Job, for example, experienced deep pain yet learned to trust God's sovereignty. Jesus Himself wept over death and injustice, showing that God is not distant from human grief.
- **Human Free Will**: Christian teaching often points out that God gave people free will, and misuse of that freedom can lead to evil actions that hurt others.
- **Hope of Restoration**: The Christian message includes the belief that God will one day set things right—ending suffering and bringing justice. In the meantime, believers can fight evil and help those who are in pain, reflecting God's compassion.
- **Walking with the Suffering**: Sometimes, the best response is not to have a neat explanation but to show empathy. Coming alongside those who hurt demonstrates Christ's love more than words alone.

Rare Perspective: Though we may not fully understand every reason for suffering now, the Bible promises that God is working toward a greater good. Faith often involves trusting God's character when we cannot see the full plan.

---

8. Dealing with Apparent Contradictions in Scripture

At times, you might stumble on verses that seem to disagree with each other, or historical details that appear conflicting.

- **Check the Context**: Many "contradictions" vanish when you read the surrounding passages, learn about the original languages, or understand the historical background.
- **Recognize Different Genres**: The Bible includes poetry, narrative, wisdom literature, prophecy, and letters. Each style can shape how a passage communicates its message.

- **Seek Scholarly Insights**: Pastors, theologians, and biblical scholars often address these puzzling passages. Research their explanations rather than assuming the Bible is flawed.
- **Practice Patience**: Some questions may remain partly unresolved due to cultural or historical distance. Being okay with "I don't fully know yet" can keep you open to learning more.

Encouraging Note: The Bible has been studied for thousands of years. If something seems confusing, it is likely that other believers have wrestled with it too. You can build on what they discovered to clarify your own understanding.

---

9. When Feelings Conflict with Beliefs

Feelings can be strong. You might know certain biblical truths, yet your heart feels differently. For example, you might feel lonely, leading you to think God has abandoned you—even though you know intellectually that God promises never to leave you.

- **Acknowledge Your Emotions**: Do not shame yourself for having strong feelings. Recognize them as part of being human.
- **Compare Feelings to Truth**: Ask, "Is my emotion telling me something that contradicts what the Bible teaches about God?" Then remind yourself of biblical promises.
- **Seek Support**: Speak with someone you trust about the clash between your heart and what you believe. They can offer perspective and emotional support.
- **Use Practical Measures**: Sometimes, physical or mental health issues can intensify negative emotions. Taking care of your body, seeking counseling, or managing stress can stabilize your mood, making it easier to trust God's truths.

Lesser-Known Tip: Some find it helpful to write biblical affirmations on sticky notes and place them where they will see them daily. Seeing these truths can counter the waves of doubt stirred by uncertain feelings.

---

10. Embracing Mystery

Christianity involves truths that may not fit into simple human logic. God is infinite, and humans are finite. Some aspects of God's nature, such as the Trinity or the idea of eternity, can stretch our understanding.

- **Welcoming Humility**: Recognize that not everything about God will be fully grasped in this life. This does not mean we stop learning, but we stay humble about our limits.
- **Appreciating Wonder**: Instead of seeing mystery as a problem, view it as something that points to a God who is greater than our minds can fully contain. This can fuel awe and worship.
- **Knowing the Essentials**: While some points might remain mysterious, key Christian beliefs—like Jesus's death and resurrection for our salvation—are clearly emphasized in Scripture. Focus on these core truths.
- **Growing Faith**: Accepting that some things remain beyond our grasp can deepen faith. You trust in a God who is bigger than your questions, not a God limited by them.

Practical Action: If you feel unsettled by theological mysteries, concentrate on what is clearly revealed—God's love, Christ's sacrifice, and the Spirit's presence. Let these anchor your faith.

---

11. How to Handle Mockery or Criticism for Having Questions

Sometimes, fellow believers might accuse you of lacking faith if you ask tough questions. On the other side, non-believers might mock you for holding Christian views. Both can be painful.

- **Stand Firm**: You have the right to ask questions about your faith without shame. Christianity invites thoughtful engagement, not blind acceptance.
- **Find Supportive Communities**: If your current circle belittles your seeking mind, look for Christian groups or mentors who value open dialogue.

- **Stay Kind**: If non-believers tease you, do not strike back. Show respect. You might surprise them with your grace under pressure.
- **Persist in Learning**: Never let criticism shut down your quest for clarity. Keep researching, praying, and seeking wise counsel.

Encouragement: Over time, your calm and genuine approach to doubt may even inspire others who have silently struggled with the same questions.

12. Biblical Encouragement for Questioning Hearts

Scripture offers many passages that can comfort you during times of doubt:

- **James 1:5**: Reminds you to ask God for wisdom, promising that He gives generously without finding fault.
- **Matthew 7:7-8**: Assures you that if you seek, you will find; if you knock, the door will be opened.
- **Mark 9:24**: The father of a possessed boy said, "I believe; help my unbelief!" This honest plea shows that partial faith combined with genuine desire can still connect you to Jesus's power.

Action Step: Pick a verse that speaks to your current struggle. Memorize or write it down. Reflect on it whenever doubt flares up.

13. Building a Lifelong Posture of Learning

Even if you resolve some doubts now, new ones may appear later. Faith is a lifetime process of growing in knowledge and trust.

- **Stay Curious**: Keep asking questions, reading books, and discussing with fellow believers. Your understanding of God's Word can deepen over the years.
- **Adapt Without Losing Core Beliefs**: You might change your views on certain secondary issues—like worship styles or interpretations of certain prophecies—as you learn more. But the core truths about Jesus should remain your foundation.

- **Share Your Journey**: By being open about your questions and how you found answers (or made peace with partial answers), you can help others who are wrestling with similar doubts.
- **Rest in God's Faithfulness**: Remember how God has guided you before. This history of faithfulness can reassure you that He will continue to lead you, even when new questions arise.

Rarely Mentioned Benefit: A faith that has faced and worked through doubts is often stronger and more personal than a faith that never asked tough questions at all.

---

14. Overcoming Paralysis by Doubt

Sometimes, repeated questions can lead you to a standstill, where you feel you cannot move forward in any direction. You might think, "I can't serve in church or share my faith until I have zero doubts." But that is not how faith typically operates.

- **Act in Faith**: Serving others, praying, and reading Scripture can all help your faith grow, even if you still have some doubts.
- **Welcome Imperfection**: You do not have to be 100% certain about every detail before being used by God. Many biblical heroes acted in spite of uncertainties.
- **Take Steps Forward**: Pick one area of service or devotion you can do wholeheartedly. Let your actions and experiences shape your faith along with your intellectual study.
- **Check Progress**: Evaluate after a while to see if your doubts have eased or changed. Sometimes, walking in obedience clarifies truth more than endless pondering.

Insight: True faith involves both heart and mind. Serving and loving people in Jesus's name can reaffirm your belief, even when certain questions remain.

---

15. Testimonies of Others Who Conquered Doubt

Hearing or reading about the real experiences of people who struggled with doubts can give you hope. Many authors, speakers, and everyday believers have shared stories of how they worked through skepticism and found their faith strengthened.

- **Biographies**: Look for stories of notable Christians who once doubted but eventually turned their questions into a deeper faith.
- **Interviews and Podcasts**: Sometimes, hearing someone's voice as they describe their journey brings extra encouragement.
- **Local Stories**: Ask older church members or leaders if they have faced big doubts. Their testimonies can show you practical ways to navigate uncertainty.

Little-Known Fact: Some people who became leading voices in Christian apologetics started out as skeptics. Their paths show that genuine searching can lead to firm conviction.

---

16. Guarding Against Cynicism

It is okay to question, but cynicism is different. Cynicism assumes the worst—believing that everything is flawed and no real truth can be found. This mindset can block genuine discovery.

- **Check Your Attitude**: Are you asking questions because you want to learn, or because you want an excuse to dismiss belief altogether?
- **Keep Hope Alive**: Remind yourself that just because some things are unclear does not mean everything is false or meaningless.
- **Stay Respectful**: Cynicism often shows up in scoffing or mocking. Instead, be open to the possibility that there are valid answers you have not encountered yet.
- **Monitor Influences**: Hanging out with extremely negative people or constantly consuming skeptical material can tilt you toward cynicism. Balance your intake with faith-building conversations and resources.

Helpful Tip: If you notice cynicism growing, take a break from certain websites or social media pages that stir up hopeless criticism. Replace them with sources that acknowledge problems while also offering constructive views.

---

17. Handling Doubt in a Community Context

Sometimes, a whole youth group or friend circle might share the same doubts. When this happens, you can tackle them together.

- **Plan Group Discussions**: Propose meeting outside of normal youth group times for deeper talks about the topic everyone is wondering about.
- **Invite a Knowledgeable Guest**: A pastor, counselor, or someone skilled in apologetics could join a discussion night to offer insights.
- **Encourage Respectful Dialogue**: Set ground rules: no mocking, no dismissing each other's points, and keep an open mind.
- **Pray as a Group**: You can ask God for wisdom as a team. This unites you and reminds you that God is the final source of truth.

Community Advantage: Sharing doubts in a group setting can reduce isolation. You realize you are not the only one who has questions, and you can collectively support one another.

---

18. Giving Yourself Time to Grow

Christian growth is often likened to a seed growing into a plant. Seeds do not sprout into full plants overnight, and neither does faith reach full maturity instantly.

- **Patience with Yourself**: You might not resolve big theological questions in a week or even a year. That is okay. Focus on steady progress.
- **Keep a Record**: Sometimes, writing down your main doubts and the steps you are taking to address them can show how far you have come.
- **Celebrate Small Victories**: If you find an explanation that makes sense or experience a deeper sense of peace about an issue, mark that step. It is evidence of growth.

- **Avoid Rushing**: Forced answers can lead to shallow faith. Allow your mind and spirit the time needed to process information and prayerfully seek understanding.

Reassuring Thought: Just as plants need sunlight, water, and time to grow strong roots, you need spiritual nourishment and patience to develop a strong faith that can handle questions.

---

19. Strengthening Your Faith Through Service

Surprisingly, engaging in practical acts of service can help you work through doubts. When you see how God's love changes lives—through feeding the hungry, comforting the lonely, or building community—it can reaffirm the core messages of Christianity.

- **Volunteering**: Join a local outreach program, help with a church mission trip, or get involved in a charity that resonates with you.
- **Small Acts of Kindness**: Even offering to babysit for a stressed parent at church or writing encouraging notes to classmates can show you how Christian values impact daily life.
- **Seeing God's Hand**: Acts of service often reveal how God uses ordinary people to spread hope. This lived experience can calm certain theological doubts.
- **Focusing on Others**: Sometimes, doubt grows when we are stuck in our own head. Serving others shifts our attention outward and can bring fresh perspective.

Powerful Reminder: You might find more clarity in the act of loving others than in simply trying to solve every puzzle academically. Christianity is both truth and practice.

---

20. Moving Forward with Confidence and Humility

Doubts and questions do not have to paralyze your faith. By facing them head-on, seeking wise counsel, and trusting that God meets honest seekers, you can emerge with a deeper, more resilient belief. Humility allows you to keep learning, while confidence grows as you see that Christianity holds up under honest inquiry.

Questions for Reflection

1. Which doubt feels most pressing to you right now, and who can you talk to about it?
2. Have you ever seen a doubt turn into a deeper understanding or a stronger faith? What did you learn from that process?
3. How can you balance an open mind with a respectful approach to Scripture and Christian teaching?

Practical Action Point
Pick one question or doubt you have. Within the next week, do something proactive about it: watch a lecture, read a book, or ask a youth leader for their take. Write down what you learn or how your perspective shifts. Even if you do not find a complete answer right away, note any progress you make.

Conclusion to Chapter 13
Questions and doubts are a natural part of any meaningful faith. Rather than hiding them, be honest with God and seek guidance from trustworthy sources. Over time, many concerns find thoughtful answers, and even if some remain partly mysterious, you can stand on the solid core of Christian truth. By staying curious, prayerful, and open, you can let your doubts push you to discover the richness of God's wisdom and love, instead of letting them pull you away from the faith that sustains you.

CHAPTER 14

Using Gifts and Talents Wisely

Introduction
Every person has unique gifts and talents. You might be great at art, music, speaking, organizing, problem-solving, caring for others, or something else entirely. Sometimes, it is easy to overlook your strengths because they come naturally to you, or to feel your gifts are too small compared to others'. However, the Bible teaches that each believer is part of the body of Christ, and each part has a special role (1 Corinthians 12).

This chapter will show how to recognize your gifts, develop them, and use them in ways that bring glory to God and help those around you. You will discover that using your talents wisely is not about showing off but about serving others and fulfilling God's plan for your life. It is a path of joy and responsibility that helps you grow and contribute to the world in a meaningful way.

---

1. Identifying Your Gifts and Talents

Some people seem to know their abilities right away. Others may take time and exploration to figure out what they are good at. Remember, gifts can be practical (like cooking, building, or organizing) or more abstract (like encouraging, teaching, or creativity).

- **Reflect on What You Enjoy**: If you often lose track of time while doing something (like playing an instrument or helping younger kids with homework), that might be a clue you have a natural talent there.
- **Ask Others**: Parents, siblings, teachers, or friends might see talents in you that you do not notice yourself.
- **Try New Activities**: You cannot know if you love public speaking unless you try it. Stepping out of your comfort zone can reveal hidden skills.
- **Pay Attention to Repeated Praise**: If multiple people remark on your art or your way of comforting people, there is likely a true skill there.

Special Note: Sometimes, the talents we ignore are the very ones God wants us to use. Stay open to possibilities, even if a talent seems ordinary.

2. Biblical Views on Talents

The Bible contains parables and teachings that mention the importance of using what God has given. One famous example is the Parable of the Talents (Matthew 25:14-30), where a master gives sums of money to his servants. Those who invest and multiply it are praised, and the one who hides it out of fear is rebuked. While this story uses money as a metaphor, it applies to any gift or ability.

- **God Values Effort and Faithfulness**: It is not just about having many gifts, but about how you use them.
- **Avoiding Fear**: Burying your abilities because you feel insecure means missing out on growth.
- **Staying Accountable**: There is a sense of responsibility to develop and share your gifts. They are not meant to remain unused.

Lesson: Even small abilities matter to God when they are used diligently. You do not need to be the most talented person around; you simply need to be faithful with what you have been given.

3. Matching Your Talents with Needs Around You

You may wonder, "How do I actually use my gift?" or "Where do I start?" Begin by looking at the needs in your community, church, or school.

- **Community Needs**: Are there local shelters needing volunteers who can cook or organize donated items? Could a youth group use a guitar player or someone to run a social media page?
- **Church Ministries**: Look at the different groups—children's ministry, worship team, tech booth, greeting team. Which one might fit your personality or skill set?
- **School Clubs**: If you are a strong writer, maybe you can help with the school newsletter. If you are athletic, consider helping a sports team or coaching younger students.
- **Online Options**: In some cases, you can use your tech abilities online—like creating graphics for a church website or offering free tutoring sessions over video calls.

Encouragement: Serving often reveals new aspects of your gifts. When you attempt something for the sake of helping, you may discover capacities you never realized you had.

---

4. Overcoming Obstacles in Using Talents

Many teens hesitate to use their abilities because of various fears. Identifying and addressing these fears can free you to step out in confidence.

- **Fear of Failure**: You may worry about messing up or not being good enough. Remember, growth often involves mistakes. Embrace them as part of the process.
- **Fear of Judgment**: You might think peers will mock you if you sing in front of people or start a project. True friends will encourage you. Even if some mock, you can lean on God's approval rather than theirs.
- **Perfectionism**: Wanting everything to be flawless can stop you from ever starting. Realize that "good enough" can still bless others, and you can improve over time.
- **Comparisons**: Seeing someone else with a similar gift might make you feel second-rate. Yet God does not compare His children. Each person's unique style and setting matter.

Rare Insight: Sometimes, doing something with a partner or small group lessens these fears. You can support each other, share ideas, and laugh off mistakes together.

---

5. Developing Your Skills with Discipline

Even natural talents need polishing. Whether you sing, paint, write, or help the elderly, discipline and practice lead to mastery.

- **Set Clear Goals**: If you play piano, aim to learn a new piece each month. If you are good at organizing, volunteer to plan small events to sharpen your coordination skills.
- **Regular Practice**: Block out time each day or week for focused improvement. Consistency is more effective than occasional bursts of effort.

- **Seek Feedback**: Ask a teacher, mentor, or more experienced friend to give you pointers. Constructive criticism can refine your abilities faster.
- **Celebrate Progress**: Recognize small improvements. This encourages you to keep going and not give up when it gets tough.

Example: Think of King David, who was skillful at playing the harp. He did not start out as an expert. He likely spent many hours practicing while tending sheep before he was called to soothe King Saul's troubled mind (1 Samuel 16:23).

---

6. Humility in Using Your Gifts

It is important to remain humble when you receive praise for what you do well. Pride can creep in and spoil the blessing of serving others.

- **Remember the Source**: Acknowledge that God gave you these talents. You did not create them from nothing.
- **Shift Focus to Others**: When you perform or succeed, think about who benefited rather than basking in attention.
- **Stay Teachable**: Even experts have room to learn. Humble leaders and performers continue honing their craft.
- **Encourage Others**: If you are recognized, use it as a chance to shine a light on teammates, collaborators, or supporters who helped you.

Biblical Warning: Proverbs 16:18 says, "Pride goes before destruction." Keeping a modest attitude protects you from arrogance and keeps your relationships healthy.

---

7. Balancing Talent Use with Daily Responsibilities

Some teens pour so much into their passions that they neglect other parts of life, like homework, chores, or family time. While nurturing talents is great, balance is key.

- **Schedule Wisely**: Use a planner to allocate time for practice, study, rest, and family. Avoid letting one area dominate all your energy.

- **Seek Accountability**: Ask parents or mentors to help you set healthy boundaries. For instance, if you love gaming design, decide how many hours a week you can devote to it without harming your schoolwork.
- **Give Yourself Breaks**: Overworking can lead to burnout, which then makes you enjoy your talents less. Short breaks can renew creativity and motivation.
- **Prioritize Relationship with God**: Make sure your quiet times of prayer and Bible reading do not get pushed aside. Your spiritual health underpins everything else.

Practical Tip: If you find yourself stressed, step back and assess your commitments. Sometimes, cutting one activity or scaling back practice sessions can restore balance and joy.

---

8. Supporting Others in Their Gifts

Part of using your talents wisely involves helping others discover and grow theirs. In God's family, we are not competitors but partners building each other up.

- **Offer Collaboration**: If you see a friend who has a gift in writing while you are good at graphic design, team up to create a short magazine or blog.
- **Give Encouragement**: Tell friends what you see them doing well. Affirming someone's ability can spark their motivation to develop it further.
- **Share Resources**: If you have access to tools, books, or connections that could help someone else, do not keep them to yourself.
- **Practice Generosity**: Sometimes, share the spotlight. If you are leading worship at church, invite another talented singer to join you on stage.

Rare Benefit: Helping others with their gifts can even refine your own. Teaching or mentoring someone can deepen your own understanding and appreciation for your craft.

9. Using Talents for Community Impact

Your gifts can be a blessing not only in church settings but also in broader communities—at school, neighborhood events, or charitable programs.

- **Public Performances**: If you have a knack for music or theater, consider local nursing homes or community centers. Many residents welcome uplifting shows or interactive events.
- **Fundraising**: Those skilled in cooking or crafts can host bake sales or craft fairs, donating proceeds to causes like missions or disaster relief funds.
- **Workshops for Younger Kids**: If you are good at soccer, reading, or basic science experiments, you can hold small workshops to teach younger kids. This builds their confidence and might spark their interests.
- **Peer Mentoring**: Offer tutoring in subjects you excel at. This improves someone's grades and gives them hope for their academic future.

Deeper Thought: When you step outside your comfort zone to serve the community, you become a role model. People see how faith in action can bring goodness to those around you, reflecting God's light in practical ways.

---

10. Avoiding Burnout and Pressure

Sometimes, people notice your gifts and keep asking for help or performances. While it is wonderful to be in demand, excessive demands can lead to burnout.

- **Set Boundaries**: It is okay to say "no" when you are overwhelmed. Politely explain that you cannot handle another commitment right now.
- **Stay in Prayer**: Ask God for guidance on which requests to accept. Not every invitation is part of His plan for you.
- **Watch for Warning Signs**: Feeling constantly exhausted, losing interest in what you once loved, or becoming resentful are signs you might be overextended.
- **Find Joy Outside Achievements**: Remember to have fun, relax, and spend time with friends or family without the pressure of performing or producing.

Key Principle: Jesus often withdrew from the crowds to rest and pray (Luke 5:16). If He needed breaks, so do you. Balancing rest and service ensures you can keep using your talents long-term.

11. Financial or Career Considerations

If your talent can be a career path, you might wonder if you should pursue it professionally. This can be an exciting but challenging decision.

- **Pray for Direction**: Ask God to open doors and give you peace if this path aligns with His will.
- **Gather Information**: Talk to people who work in that field. Learn about the training, job market, and daily responsibilities.
- **Check Your Motives**: Do you want to do this work to serve others and honor God, or only to gain fame or wealth? It is good to examine your heart.
- **Stay Flexible**: You can use your gifts in multiple ways. If you do not get your dream job right away, you can still volunteer or have side projects that express your abilities.

Example: A gifted singer might eventually record music or lead worship full-time, but she could also use her skill in part-time gigs, volunteer events, or local church ministries. Both routes can be meaningful.

---

12. Dealing with Jealousy and Competition

Seeing others excel in a similar talent can stir jealousy. You might think, "She's better at singing than I am. What if people like her more?" Such comparisons can harm friendships and hinder your joy.

- **Recall Each Person's Uniqueness**: God has diverse ways of using different voices, styles, or approaches. One singer might excel in classical music, another in gospel. Both can serve beautifully.
- **Acknowledge Their Success**: Congratulate them genuinely. Showing happiness for others can reduce envy and build stronger bonds.
- **Focus on Your Journey**: Keep improving your skills and trust God's timing for recognition or opportunities.
- **Pray for a Loving Heart**: If jealousy creeps in, ask God to fill you with love, humility, and a desire to see others thrive.

Practical Step: When you feel envy, try doing something kind for the person you are envying. It shifts your mindset from competition to support.

13. Serving the Church Body Together

When believers come together, combining their talents, the church can run smoothly and reach out to the world more effectively.

- **Complementary Roles**: Someone gifted in teaching can lead Bible studies, another skilled in tech can manage sound systems, and a creative person can design event posters.
- **Special Occasions**: Christmas or Easter events often need drama, music, set design, hospitality, and so on. Everyone's talents can join to present a memorable program.
- **Mission Trips**: Whether local or overseas, a trip might require language skills, construction abilities, medical knowledge, or simply a welcoming spirit.
- **Ongoing Ministries**: Soup kitchens, Sunday schools, worship teams, and visitation programs are just a few areas that constantly need dedicated workers.

Encouragement: Working as a team allows you to see God's design in action. Not all are called to preach; some serve by quietly cleaning or organizing. Each role is valuable.

14. Staying Faithful in Small Tasks

Sometimes, you might think your abilities are not special enough to matter. But the Bible reminds us that even seemingly small acts are significant in God's eyes.

- **Greeting People**: If you have a friendly personality, being a church greeter sets a warm tone for newcomers.
- **Babysitting**: Freeing parents to attend a Bible study can be a big gift. It also hones your responsibility skills.
- **Making Cards**: Handwritten notes for the elderly or sick can brighten their day. If you are artistic, this becomes a heartfelt way to use your creativity.

- **Maintenance**: Sweeping floors, changing lightbulbs, or updating the church bulletin board may not grab attention, but they keep the environment welcoming.

Quiet Fact: Jesus praised the widow who gave two small coins because she gave from her heart (Mark 12:41-44). Your small talent, used faithfully, can please God just as much as a grand performance.

---

15. Keeping God at the Center

As you develop and use your talents, never lose sight of the One who gave them to you. Maintaining a strong connection with God ensures your efforts remain aligned with His purposes.

- **Daily Devotions**: A short time of prayer or Bible reading keeps you spiritually grounded.
- **Ask for Guidance**: Before a performance or service project, pray for God to work through you and to protect you from pride.
- **Thank God for Progress**: When you notice improvement in your skills or a good response from others, give God the credit.
- **Stay Attuned to His Leading**: Sometimes, God nudges you to step away from one opportunity to open the door for another. Obeying these promptings shows trust in His bigger plan.

Reassuring Thought: You are a steward of the gifts God has lent you. By staying close to Him, you make wise choices and avoid misusing your abilities.

---

16. Examples of Teens Using Their Talents

Many teenagers have done remarkable things by applying their gifts. Some start non-profit groups, create inspirational content online, or develop clubs that address real needs. You can find stories of teens who:

- **Raised Money**: Using their baking or music skills to support missions or community causes.

- **Led Younger Kids**: Coaching sports teams, teaching Sunday school, or creating clubs for children after school.
- **Innovated**: Designing helpful apps, producing Christian music tracks, or writing encouraging blog posts.
- **Encouraged Their Peers**: Launching support groups for classmates who struggle with stress or personal issues, drawing on empathy and organizational talents.

Motivation: Hearing about other teens can spark ideas for how you might step out. It also reminds you that you do not have to wait until adulthood to make a real difference.

---

17. Dealing with Changing or Multiple Talents

You might find your interests and abilities shift over time. Perhaps you used to be enthusiastic about drawing but now feel drawn to photography. Or you might have multiple talents and feel torn.

- **Stay Flexible**: God may guide you through seasons. One skill might be for a certain stage, and another could emerge later.
- **Combine Talents**: For instance, if you love both music and technology, you could help record and mix worship songs. If you enjoy cooking and speaking, you could host a cooking class that includes a short inspirational talk.
- **Test the Waters**: If you sense a new interest, try it out in small ways before committing fully. This helps you see if it is truly a calling or just a fleeting curiosity.
- **Seek Counsel**: Talk with people who know you well. They can help you discern whether you are being pulled in too many directions or if these talents can work together.

Reassurance: Having multiple gifts can be a blessing, not a burden. The key is to use them wisely, not to get overwhelmed by wanting to do everything at once.

18. Inviting Others to Partner with You

Using your gifts does not mean doing everything by yourself. Collaboration often amplifies what you can accomplish.

- **Form a Team**: If you have a vision—like starting a youth worship night—recruit friends who can handle sound setup, promotion, or welcoming guests.
- **Appreciate Differing Views**: A friend might have a different style of creativity or approach. Working together can produce a richer result than going solo.
- **Keep Communication Clear**: Talk openly about responsibilities, deadlines, and goals. Good teamwork prevents misunderstandings and conflicts.
- **Share Joys and Burdens**: Celebrate successes together, and pray or strategize when challenges arise. A supportive team stands stronger.

Practical Thought: Team projects can sharpen your talents because you learn from each other's strengths. You also practice leadership and gain experience in real-world collaboration, which helps for future careers or ministries.

---

19. Guarding Against Prideful Competition

While healthy comparison can inspire you to grow, prideful competition can harm relationships and your spiritual well-being.

- **Avoid Showing Off**: If your aim is to make everyone see how talented you are, you might lose the heart of serving God and others.
- **Cheer for Peers**: If a friend outperforms you, be happy for them. Do not let envy spoil your friendship or your own passion.
- **Stay Rooted in Purpose**: Remind yourself why you began using your gift: to bless people, honor God, or express creativity. That reason should outweigh chasing applause.
- **Reflect Regularly**: Ask yourself if you are being motivated by pride or service. Quick heart checks can prevent bigger problems.

Biblical Note: Philippians 2:3 urges believers to "do nothing out of selfish ambition or vain conceit." This humility fosters real unity and joy in shared service.

20. Moving Forward with Confidence and Purpose

Using your gifts and talents wisely is a wonderful way to serve God and people. It fosters personal growth, strengthens your community, and shows the world the creativity and love God placed in you. Do not be afraid to test new areas, refine your skills, and get involved in projects that stretch you. Keep your eyes on God, stay humble, and remember that every bit of service—big or small—counts in His Kingdom.

Questions for Reflection

1. Which personal strengths or gifts do you think you might be overlooking?
2. What practical steps can you take this month to develop or use a talent more effectively?
3. How can you encourage a friend who seems unaware of their God-given abilities?

Practical Action Point
Pick one talent you have identified. Make a short plan—maybe just three steps—to use it for good in the next four weeks. For example, if you are good at writing, commit to creating a short devotional for your youth group or write letters to patients at a local hospital. Track your progress, note what you learn, and see how God works through your actions.

Conclusion to Chapter 14
God gave you unique abilities for a reason. Whether you are skilled in art, leadership, care for people, or any other area, you can use those gifts to serve, uplift, and honor Him. Your talents are not just for your own benefit; they also bring hope, joy, and support to those around you. As you move forward, keep refining your skills, helping others, and thanking God for the ways He can work through you. When you do, you will find deep fulfillment and see how even the smallest offering can be multiplied for great impact.

CHAPTER 15

Developing Self-Control

Introduction
Self-control is an important quality for anyone wanting to live with purpose and positive influence. For Christian teen girls, self-control involves managing emotions, desires, and actions in a way that reflects faith in God. It can affect many areas of life: what you watch, how you speak, the friendships you keep, and even how you handle school responsibilities. While the process can be challenging, growing in self-control can bring freedom rather than restriction. It helps you avoid unwise decisions and builds strength in character.

In this chapter, you will learn practical tips to develop self-control that align with biblical principles. This includes acknowledging triggers that test your patience, setting clear personal guidelines, and finding ways to rely on God for strength. You will also see that small daily choices can lead to big changes in how you handle temptations and pressures.

---

1. Understanding What Self-Control Really Means

Self-control is the ability to guide your thoughts, actions, and words according to what is right, rather than just reacting to feelings or outside pressures. It does not mean denying yourself all good things. Instead, it is about putting your long-term well-being and faith values above short-term impulses.

- **Not Just Willpower**: While willpower is part of it, real self-control also involves wisdom and spiritual help. Human willpower alone might fade when feelings get intense or when pressure is huge.
- **More Than Avoiding Mistakes**: True self-control leads you to choose what is beneficial, not just to avoid something harmful.
- **A Sign of Maturity**: As you grow, you learn to think before speaking or acting. This careful approach can prevent regret and foster healthier relationships.

Helpful Thought: Picture self-control as a guard at the gate of your heart and mind, checking what enters and leaves. This guard ensures only good and uplifting things pass through, protecting you from harmful influences and poor decisions.

2. Why Self-Control Can Be Hard

Many teens struggle with self-control because emotions and peer pressures can be very strong. Biology also plays a role—adolescent years are marked by changes in the brain that can make impulsive reactions more common. Plus, modern technology, with constant notifications and instant content, can make distractions more tempting than ever.

- **Strong Emotions**: Feeling upset, excited, or disappointed can lead to quick reactions without thinking.
- **Influences Everywhere**: Ads, social media, and peers might urge you to chase trends or indulge in habits that clash with your values.
- **Fear of Missing Out**: Sometimes, you might give in to impulses because you do not want to feel left out or behind others who seem to be enjoying themselves.

Key Point: Recognizing these challenges is the first step. You are not "weak" for finding self-control difficult; you are human. The good news is that, with the right tools and support, you can grow stronger in this area.

3. Biblical Insights on Self-Control

Scripture addresses self-control quite a bit, showing that God recognizes its importance in our daily lives.

- **Fruit of the Spirit**: Galatians 5:22-23 lists self-control as part of the "fruit" produced by the Holy Spirit in believers. This suggests that as you stay connected to God, He helps you grow in self-control.
- **Examples of Self-Control**: Joseph in the Old Testament resisted temptation by fleeing from Potiphar's wife (Genesis 39). Daniel chose not to eat the king's food that violated his beliefs (Daniel 1). Both showed restraint guided by their faith.

- **Warnings Against Lack of Control**: Proverbs 25:28 says a person without self-control is like a city without walls. In ancient times, walls protected a city. Likewise, self-control protects your life from chaos.

Encouragement: Self-control is not a modern concept. Believers throughout history have needed it to honor God. You can draw on these examples and biblical teachings for motivation.

---

4. Recognizing Your Triggers

A "trigger" is something that makes you more likely to lose control—whether that is losing patience, indulging in a bad habit, or saying something unkind. Identifying triggers helps you plan ways to respond differently.

- **Emotional Triggers**: Stress, anxiety, or anger might lower your guard. If you know a certain topic or environment sets you off, you can plan to stay calm or avoid that situation if possible.
- **People Triggers**: Certain friends or social circles might pressure you toward unhealthy choices. This does not mean you must cut them out, but you should set limits or have strategies for saying no.
- **Environmental Triggers**: Time of day, location, or even hunger and tiredness can affect your willpower. Late nights, for example, might be a time you are more prone to watch or do things you later regret.

Practical Exercise: Keep a small journal and note situations when you lose control. Write what happened, how you felt, and what you think triggered it. Over time, patterns may emerge, guiding you to make changes.

---

5. Setting Personal Guidelines

Clear guidelines provide structure when you need to make quick decisions. These can relate to social media use, phone time, what you watch, or even daily schedules.

- **Time Boundaries**: Decide how much time you will spend on social media or gaming. Use built-in app timers or ask a friend to keep you accountable.
- **Moral Boundaries**: For instance, if you value purity, establish how far is too far in a dating relationship. Or if you want to speak kindly, set a rule for yourself to avoid any mean teasing.
- **Spiritual Boundaries**: You might commit to reading a small portion of the Bible daily and praying before bed, so other activities do not crowd it out.
- **Healthy Routines**: Plan bedtime and wake-up times to ensure you get enough rest. Tiredness can weaken your self-control the next day.

Note: These guidelines are not supposed to be rigid rules that rob your freedom. They serve as guardrails, helping you stay on track with your larger goals and values.

---

6. Using Accountability

Accountability means you agree to share your progress or struggles with a trustworthy person. This person checks in, encourages you, and may even correct you gently if you step off track.

- **Find Someone You Respect**: A mature friend, older sibling, youth leader, or parent can fulfill this role if they are supportive and understanding.
- **Set Clear Expectations**: Explain your goals, like "I want to spend only one hour a day on social media" or "I want to avoid saying mean jokes." Then ask them to check on you at set times.
- **Be Honest**: Accountability only works if you tell the truth. Hiding mistakes out of shame defeats the point.
- **Mark Progress**: When you succeed for a day, a week, or a month, let your accountability partner know. Their encouragement can keep you going.

Rare Tip: You can also have a mutual accountability arrangement with a friend who has similar goals. You both hold each other to your commitments, making the process more balanced.

7. Practical Ways to Resist Temptation

When temptations flare up, you need quick strategies to handle them. Whether it is resisting negative speech, gossip, unhealthy media, or overindulging in junk food, here are helpful tools:

- **Distraction**: Shift your attention to something else for a few minutes—do a simple chore, read a short Bible verse, or text a positive friend. Often, the urge fades if you do not feed it.
- **Positive Replacement**: Replace the unhealthy action with a healthier one. For example, if you want to watch something questionable, instead watch a wholesome video or step outside for fresh air.
- **Memorized Scripture**: Recalling a relevant Bible verse can bring clarity in a tempting moment. If you struggle with anger, memorizing James 1:19 ("be quick to listen, slow to speak, and slow to become angry") can remind you to pause.
- **Physical Removal**: If possible, physically remove yourself from the tempting environment. Turn off your device, leave the room, or walk away from a tense situation before saying something you regret.

Point to Remember: Temptations usually pass if you do not surrender immediately. Each second you wait, you build your self-control muscles.

---

8. Handling Digital Distractions

Smartphones, streaming services, and the internet can easily pull you away from tasks or healthy limits. These digital tools are not bad in themselves, but without boundaries, they can erode self-control.

- **App Limits**: Many phones have settings to limit time on specific apps. Use them. If you exceed your limit, the app is locked unless you deliberately override it.
- **Scheduled Disconnect**: Pick blocks of time—maybe an hour before bed or during homework—when you keep your phone off or in another room.
- **Quiet Mode**: Turn off notifications that are not essential. Constant pings can break your focus and make you crave immediate responses.

- **Use Technology for Accountability**: Some apps report your screen time to a friend or parent. Knowing someone else sees how you spend your time online can encourage responsible use.

Deep Thought: Technology is a tool, not a master. Letting it rule your day can weaken your resolve, but controlling it can free you to reach more fulfilling goals.

---

9. Building Good Mental Habits

Self-control includes the mind. If your thoughts spiral into negativity or overthinking, it is harder to remain calm and choose wisely. Practice guiding your internal dialogue.

- **Positive Self-Talk**: Instead of saying "I can't handle this," say "I can do this with God's help" or "I can try my best even if it's tough."
- **Thinking Before Reacting**: When something upsets you, train yourself to pause, count to five, or take a deep breath. This small delay can prevent harsh words or hasty decisions.
- **Focusing on Solutions**: If a problem arises, quickly shift your mind from complaints to potential fixes. This approach can defuse worry and lead to action.
- **Gratefulness**: Listing what you are thankful for each day can break cycles of complaining or self-pity. It also reminds you of God's faithfulness.

Practical Exercise: Each night, review your day's thoughts. Did you dwell on negativity or panic, or did you try to stay hopeful? This awareness can guide tomorrow's improvements.

---

10. Learning from Mistakes Without Giving Up

No one is perfect. You will slip sometimes—maybe you snap at a sibling or go on a social media binge. The key is to learn and keep moving forward rather than sinking into shame.

- **Admit the Mistake**: Acknowledge what happened without making excuses. Reflect on why it happened.
- **Apologize if Needed**: If your lack of control hurt someone else, say sorry sincerely. Trying to fix the harm can prevent lingering guilt.
- **Look for the Cause**: Were you tired, stressed, or triggered by something specific? This helps you plan a better response next time.
- **Reset**: Remind yourself that God's mercies are new every morning (Lamentations 3:22-23). Start fresh, carrying lessons from the stumble but not letting it define you.

Encouragement: Mistakes are often the best teachers. Each time you fail, you gain insight that can help you stand stronger in the future.

---

11. Balancing Self-Control with Healthy Emotions

Having self-control does not mean suppressing all emotions. Emotions are part of life and can guide you to important truths. The goal is to feel them without letting them drive you off-course.

- **Allowing Emotions**: If you feel sad, it is okay to cry or talk about it. If you are happy, it is fine to laugh. Acknowledge feelings without shame.
- **Regulating Responses**: The difference is you do not let anger lead to hurtful speech or jealousy lead to mean behavior. You learn to pause and choose a wise reaction.
- **Using Emotions for Good**: Anger over injustice can motivate you to volunteer or speak up for someone being bullied. Sadness can help you develop empathy for others who are hurting.
- **Praying Through Feelings**: Sharing emotions with God can bring comfort and clarity. You might find that He calms your heart and provides perspective.

Rare Tip: Picture emotions as signals on a dashboard, telling you something about your internal state. They are valuable but should not grab the steering wheel of your decisions.

12. Drawing on God's Strength

Human effort has limits. In times when controlling yourself seems nearly impossible, lean on God's power through prayer and faith.

- **Asking for Help**: A simple prayer like, "Lord, help me stay calm" or "Give me wisdom in this moment" can shift your perspective immediately.
- **Remembering Bible Promises**: Verses like Philippians 4:13 ("I can do all things through Christ who strengthens me") remind you that divine help is available.
- **Trusting the Holy Spirit**: According to Galatians 5:22-23, self-control is a spiritual fruit. This means the Holy Spirit can produce it in you if you remain open and yielded.
- **Practicing Reliance**: Make it a habit to turn to God throughout the day, not just in crisis. Consistent reliance fosters deeper spiritual maturity.

Encouragement: When you face a tough temptation, remember you are not alone. God cares and can supply the inner resolve you need.

---

13. Building Self-Control in Specific Areas

Let's consider a few common areas where teen girls often want more self-control:

1. **Eating Habits**: Balancing nutrition is key. Eat a variety of foods, but watch out for emotional eating. If stress makes you grab junk food, find healthier stress outlets like a brisk walk or a quick prayer break.
2. **Speech**: Gossip, rude jokes, and foul language can slip out easily. Train yourself to pause before speaking. If you cannot say something kind or true, practice holding back.
3. **Time Management**: Procrastination leads to last-minute stress. Plan study sessions, set smaller goals, and reward yourself when tasks are completed on time.
4. **Technology Use**: As covered earlier, set limits. Remove apps if they are too tempting and keep your phone away during classes or devotions.
5. **Personal Boundaries**: In dating or friendships, self-control might mean maintaining respectful physical or emotional limits. Know your standards and do not let momentary feelings override them.

Practical Tip: Pick one area to work on first. Focus on small, consistent changes. Once you see progress, move on to another area.

---

14. Involving Family and Friends

Your closest circle can either undermine or support your effort to develop self-control. Invite them into your growth process.

- **Explain Your Goals**: Let parents or siblings know you want to speak more kindly or manage screen time better. They can remind you gently if they see you slipping.
- **Create Joint Habits**: For instance, if you want to keep phones out of the bedroom at night, encourage everyone in your home to do the same.
- **Encourage Two-Way Support**: If a friend also wants to grow in self-control, you can exchange ideas and cheer each other on. This bonding can make the process more fun.
- **Handle Criticism Calmly**: If family members tease you or do not believe you will change, stay polite and keep working on your goals. Over time, your consistent efforts might change their opinions.

Hidden Benefit: Having a supportive environment multiplies your motivation. Plus, as you improve, you become a good role model to those around you.

---

15. Facing Peer Pressure to Break Boundaries

Sometimes, people around you may mock your self-control choices. They might say you are too strict or missing out on "fun." Yet staying true to your convictions can strengthen your character in the long run.

- **Polite Decline**: Learn simple phrases like, "No thanks, I'm not into that" or "I already have other plans." You do not owe a lengthy explanation if someone tries to push you.
- **Confident Nonchalance**: Show you are not ashamed of your decision. If you act embarrassed, it may fuel more teasing. If you act calm, people often lose interest in pressuring you.

- **Select Friends Wisely**: Over time, gravitate toward those who respect your decisions. You can maintain kindness to everyone, but you do not have to let people consistently undermine your values.
- **Reflect on the Consequences**: Peer pressure often leads to regrets later. Reminding yourself of possible outcomes can keep you resolute.

Deep Thought: Real friends understand and support your path of growth. If someone only likes you when you break your standards, they may not value the real you.

---

16. Guarding Your Spiritual Life

Spiritual discipline can boost your self-control in every other aspect of life. Spending time with God adjusts your mindset and strengthens your moral foundation.

- **Prayer Routine**: Even a few minutes each morning or evening sets the tone for the day, helping you respond with grace in moments of temptation.
- **Scripture Meditation**: Think about Bible verses that speak to self-control or other character qualities. Let them shape your thinking.
- **Regular Fellowship**: Attending church and youth group can keep you accountable and inspired. Hearing sermons or testimonies may spark new commitment to your goals.
- **Worship and Thankfulness**: Singing or listening to praise music can calm your heart. Recognizing God's goodness fills you with a sense of purpose that outweighs impulsive desires.

Encouragement: The closer you are to God, the clearer your boundaries become. His guidance can also comfort you when you face struggles, reminding you that He cares about your growth.

---

17. Step-by-Step Growth Plan

If you feel overwhelmed by the idea of self-control, break it into smaller steps:

1. **Pick One Area**: Identify a specific behavior you want to improve—like cutting down negative talk or spending too much time on Netflix.
2. **Set a Short-Term Goal**: For example, "This week, I will keep my TV or streaming time to 30 minutes a day."
3. **Track Progress**: Use a habit tracker or note it in a journal. Each time you stick to the goal, mark it.
4. **Adjust as Needed**: If 30 minutes is too strict or too easy, tweak it. The aim is gradual improvement, not perfect success overnight.
5. **Reward Yourself**: Plan a simple treat after a week of success—like reading a favorite book or taking a relaxing bath. Acknowledge the small victory.
6. **Add Another Habit**: Once the first improvement feels natural, pick a new area to tackle.

Rare Tip: Sometimes combining a spiritual practice with your self-control goal helps. For instance, pray briefly whenever you finish a day meeting your limit, thanking God for helping you.

---

18. Handling Stress without Losing Control

Stress is a big factor that can weaken your resolve. When overwhelmed, you might lash out, skip boundaries, or seek quick comfort in unwise ways.

- **Know Your Stress Signs**: Headaches, irritability, or constant worry can indicate you are under too much pressure.
- **Healthy Outlets**: Activities like jogging, journaling, listening to uplifting music, or talking to a trusted adult can release tension.
- **Time Management**: Being organized reduces last-minute panic that leads to meltdown moments.
- **Call on God**: In stress, remember Philippians 4:6-7 about praying instead of being anxious. This doesn't fix everything instantly, but it can bring inner calm and better choices.

Practical Suggestion: Next time you sense stress building, pause and take three slow breaths. Ask God for a calm spirit. This short practice can prevent an emotional blow-up.

---

19. Long-Term Benefits of Self-Control

It might feel tough now, but self-control reaps deep rewards over time:

- **Better Health**: You avoid extreme behaviors and take care of your body.
- **Stronger Relationships**: People trust someone who is consistent and measured in reactions.
- **Greater Opportunities**: Teachers, coaches, or mentors notice students who manage themselves well, opening doors for leadership roles or scholarships.
- **Growth in Faith**: As you align your habits with biblical principles, your bond with God deepens.

Reassurance: Habits formed in your teen years often stay with you into adulthood. By working on self-control now, you set yourself up for a more confident, stable future.

---

20. Looking Ahead

Developing self-control is an ongoing process. Each day offers fresh chances to practice patience, moderation, and healthy boundaries. You will stumble at times, but the key is to keep going, relying on God and learning from each slip. Through consistent steps, you will discover that self-control brings freedom—a calmness in decision-making, a sense of responsibility in actions, and a stronger connection to the faith you hold dear.

Questions for Reflection

1. Which area of your life do you most want to improve in terms of self-control right now?
2. What triggers have you noticed that make it hard to stay disciplined?
3. Who could you ask to be an accountability partner?

Practical Action Point
Choose one habit that you feel is getting out of control—maybe snacking late at night or spending too much time on a phone app. For the next two weeks, commit to a daily limit or replacement strategy. Write down each day if you meet your goal. At the end, reflect on how it affected your mood, health, or relationships. Adjust as needed, and remember to ask God for strength.

CHAPTER 16

Helping Others in the Community

Introduction
Serving the community is a powerful way to show kindness and put Christian love into action. For a teen girl who follows Christ, helping others is not just a nice idea; it is part of living out your faith. The Bible often highlights care for the needy and for those who cannot help themselves. When you step beyond your personal concerns and give time or resources to benefit others, you spread hope and can even gain valuable life lessons.

This chapter will explore practical ways to serve different groups—such as neighbors, the elderly, the homeless, and those facing tough challenges. You will learn how to find local needs, gather support from friends or church members, and make a lasting impact. You will also see that serving others does not require grand gestures. Small acts of help, done with sincerity, can brighten someone's day and show them God's love in a personal way.

---

1. Why Serving Matters

At the heart of Christianity is the example of Jesus, who washed His disciples' feet and taught that those who help the "least of these" are actually serving Him (Matthew 25:40). If you want to grow in faith, one of the most direct ways is to look around and see who you can help.

- **Reflects God's Heart**: God cares deeply for the vulnerable. By helping them, you mirror His compassion.
- **Builds Humility and Gratitude**: Seeing other people's struggles can remind you to appreciate your blessings and approach life with a gentler attitude.
- **Strengthens Community Bonds**: Helping your neighbors or those in your school fosters unity. People become more connected, and loneliness decreases.
- **Spiritual Growth**: Serving can deepen your relationship with God as you rely on His guidance and experience the joy of giving without expecting anything in return.

Deep Thought: Instead of waiting until you feel "ready," take small steps of service now. God often works powerfully through ordinary moments and everyday acts of kindness.

---

2. Identifying Local Needs

Before jumping into action, find out what your community truly needs. This helps you use your time wisely, matching your resources with real problems.

- **Observe Your Surroundings**: Pay attention when walking in your neighborhood. Do you see litter, abandoned spaces, or people who seem lonely?
- **Check Community Notices**: Look at local bulletin boards, online groups, or church announcements. They might list volunteer opportunities or highlight families in need.
- **Ask Around**: Chat with neighbors, teachers, or church leaders. Ask if there are any known cases of students who need help, families struggling, or community events in need of volunteers.
- **Assess Your Skills**: If you are good at tutoring, you might help classmates or younger kids. If you like cooking, prepare meals for a local shelter. If you have a caring personality, visiting an elderly person might be a fit.

Practical Tip: Make a short list of three to five potential areas of need you notice. Then pick one to start with. Focusing on a single issue keeps you from feeling overwhelmed.

---

3. Simple Acts of Neighborly Kindness

Your neighbors are the closest individuals you can help. Acts of kindness do not always need an official program or large event.

- **Greeting Cards**: Make or buy small cards to leave on neighbors' doors—especially those who are sick or older. A kind note can mean a lot.
- **Yard Work**: If an older neighbor struggles with yard tasks, offer to mow their lawn or rake leaves. If you have younger siblings, involve them too.

- **Baked Goods**: Surprise a neighbor with cookies or muffins. Check for dietary needs first. This small gesture can open conversation and friendship.
- **Pet Care**: If a neighbor goes on vacation, offering to feed or walk their pet can be a big help.

Lesser-Known Insight: These small efforts build trust and respect in a neighborhood. People may be more willing to help you in return if you ever face a problem, creating a supportive environment for everyone.

4. Volunteering at Local Organizations

Various organizations welcome teen volunteers. Your involvement can add fresh energy and perspective while giving you hands-on experience.

- **Food Banks**: They often need help sorting donations, packing boxes, or distributing goods to clients.
- **Libraries**: Some libraries have youth volunteer programs for reshelving books, assisting at events, or reading to younger kids.
- **Animal Shelters**: If you love animals, shelters may need help cleaning cages, walking dogs, or socializing cats.
- **Nursing Homes**: Visiting residents, helping with crafts, or simply talking with them can combat loneliness.
- **Community Centers**: They may host after-school programs where you can mentor younger students or help with sports.

Rare Benefit: Volunteering can also expose you to different career paths. You may discover new interests or skills while serving.

5. Organizing a Group Project

Sometimes, gathering a few friends or youth group members can accomplish larger tasks. Working as a team also bonds you with people who share your passion to serve.

- **Identify a Project**: Maybe your school yard is messy, or a local park is in disrepair. It could be painting an old fence or planting flowers.
- **Delegate Roles**: Each person can contribute differently—some handle logistics, others gather supplies, and another manages communication.
- **Fundraise if Needed**: If you require materials, you can hold a bake sale or do a car wash to cover costs.
- **Request Local Support**: Let neighbors or community leaders know what you plan. They might donate paint or supplies, or even join in.

Key Point: Leading a group project teaches leadership, communication, and problem-solving. Even a small-scale project can make a noticeable difference.

---

6. Helping the Homeless

Seeing people without homes can stir compassion, but it is easy to feel unsure how to help. Simple, consistent acts often have a real impact.

- **Care Packages**: Assemble small kits with toiletries, socks, and healthy snacks. Give them to homeless individuals or donate them to shelters.
- **Serving at a Shelter**: Many shelters allow volunteers to help serve meals. This offers a chance to interact and learn about each person's situation.
- **Drives for Essential Items**: Ask your church or school if you can host a coat or blanket drive before winter. Warm clothing can literally save lives in cold weather.
- **Be Kind**: Smile or say hello if you pass someone on the street. Even if you cannot give money, acknowledging their humanity can help them feel less invisible.

Deep Thought: Homelessness often has complex causes, like job loss or health issues. Showing empathy and compassion can shift your perspective, reminding you that each person has a story.

---

7. Spending Time with the Elderly

Older adults can sometimes feel forgotten or lonely, especially if they have lost mobility or have fewer family visits. Visiting or assisting them can bring warmth and connection.

- **Regular Visits**: Commit to dropping by a local nursing home once a week. Read a book to someone, listen to their stories, or just chat.
- **Help with Technology**: Many elderly folks want to learn basic computer or smartphone tasks. Teaching them can help them keep in touch with distant family.
- **Celebrate Birthdays**: Organize a small get-together. Even if it is just a balloon and a homemade card, acknowledging their special day means a lot.
- **Yard or House Assistance**: If an older neighbor still lives at home, offer to help with chores. Shoveling snow or cleaning gutters can be tough for them.

Rare Note: Building friendships across generations broadens your understanding of life. Listening to their wisdom can also help you avoid repeating mistakes and appreciate simpler joys.

---

8. Tutoring or Mentoring Younger Kids

If you do well in school or have a skill in sports or arts, sharing that knowledge can boost someone's confidence and open new doors for them.

- **Homework Help**: Talk to a teacher or guidance counselor to find younger students struggling with subjects you enjoy. Offer after-school tutoring once a week.
- **Reading Buddies**: Libraries or elementary schools often have reading buddy programs where older students help younger ones practice reading.
- **Skills Sessions**: If you are good at soccer or drawing, hold a basic workshop for children. It is both fun and informative.
- **Ongoing Mentorship**: Keep track of a younger kid's progress, check in regularly, and encourage them to stay on track with their goals.

Hidden Bonus: Teaching someone else often strengthens your own knowledge. You also learn patience, empathy, and leadership skills in the process.

---

9. Supporting Peers in Tough Situations

The community includes people your own age who might be dealing with crises: bullying, family problems, or health issues. You can help in practical ways.

- **Listening Ear**: Sometimes, being available to hear them out—without judging—can lift a big emotional weight.
- **Study Group**: If a classmate is falling behind due to stress or a health issue, invite them to a small study group. Encouraging them academically can prevent them from giving up.
- **Resource Guidance**: Point them to counselors, youth pastors, or hotlines if the situation is serious. Know the local or school-based resources to guide them safely.
- **Positive Presence**: In a school environment, showing kindness daily (like sitting with someone who is alone) can reduce feelings of isolation.

Key Reminder: You are not called to fix everyone's problems on your own, but you can be a bridge to hope, showing empathy and practical support.

---

10. Balancing Service with Your Own Needs

It is crucial to avoid burnout. Serving is good, but neglecting personal responsibilities, mental health, or spiritual life can lead to negative effects.

- **Set Limits**: Decide how much time you can realistically give each week. It might be a few hours on Saturday or short, consistent sessions on weekdays.
- **Quality Over Quantity**: Doing a few projects thoroughly is better than many half-finished ones. Make sure you can follow through on what you promise.
- **Self-Care**: Rest, prayer, and recreation are not selfish—they refuel you so you can serve effectively.
- **Ask for Help**: If a project grows too large, recruit friends, church members, or classmates to share the load.

Advice: Jesus often withdrew to quiet places to pray after helping crowds. If He took time to recharge, you can too.

11. Teaming Up with Your Church

Church communities can be great partners in service. They may already have outreach programs or resources that can support your ideas.

- **Youth Group Projects**: Suggest an idea—like a trip to a food bank or a Sunday afternoon serving the elderly—and see if the youth leader can help arrange it.
- **Mission Opportunities**: Some churches plan short-term local or international trips. If you feel ready, this could be a unique way to serve and learn about different cultures.
- **Holiday Outreach**: Churches often collect items for Thanksgiving or Christmas baskets for needy families. Join the effort or offer to organize some part of it.
- **Sharing Testimonies**: If you already volunteer somewhere, ask your pastor if you can briefly talk about it in service. Others might be inspired to join.

Benefit: Working with a church group means more hands, shared motivation, and prayer support to keep the project focused on glorifying God rather than personal pride.

---

12. Considering Online Ways to Help

In a digital era, not all community service is done face-to-face. Some organizations operate online or need virtual help.

- **Virtual Tutoring**: Platforms connect you with kids from different areas who need homework help or English practice.
- **Social Media Awareness**: If there is a cause you care about—like mental health or anti-bullying—sharing balanced facts or positive messages can help spread hope.
- **Fundraising Pages**: You can set up a small campaign for a trusted charity. While being careful with safety and transparency, you can invite friends to donate.
- **Encouragement Online**: Posting uplifting content or messaging a struggling peer can be a form of service. Just be sure to maintain healthy boundaries and privacy rules.

Caution: Always verify online charities or platforms for credibility to avoid scams. Also, balance screen time with real-life connections.

---

13. Learning New Skills Through Service

Serving others is not just about giving—it can also teach you valuable lessons. The process may strengthen your leadership, empathy, or organizational skills.

- **Communication**: Explaining a project to others or requesting donations helps you speak clearly and politely.
- **Budgeting**: If you raise money or buy supplies, you will learn how to handle funds responsibly.
- **Time Management**: Balancing service with school and family life forces you to plan carefully.
- **Problem-Solving**: Unexpected issues (like bad weather on the day of an event) teach you to adapt and stay calm under pressure.

Positive Side Effect: Such experiences can also look good on college or scholarship applications, showing you are proactive and caring.

---

14. Showing Respect to Those You Serve

Dignity is vital. When you help someone, do it in a way that respects their worth and does not make them feel like a project.

- **Listen First**: Ask about their needs rather than assuming you know. You might discover that a shy student needs emotional support more than homework help.
- **Offer Choices**: If you are giving items to someone in need, let them pick what suits them, rather than forcing your preferences.
- **Avoid Pity**: Approach them as equals. You are not "above" anyone because you are helping. You are just using your resources or time to uplift them.
- **Keep Privacy**: If you share about your service on social media, ask permission first. Some people may not want their situation publicly displayed.

Important Reminder: Everyone has dignity, as they are created in God's image. Genuine help comes with kindness and understanding, not a sense of superiority.

---

15. Staying Consistent Rather Than One-Time Only

While a single act of kindness is great, continuous involvement can create deeper change and more meaningful relationships.

- **Weekly or Monthly Commitment**: If you volunteer regularly at a shelter or center, you build trust with people there. They know you are reliable and truly care.
- **Follow Up**: If you help an elderly neighbor once, check on them again in a few weeks. Long-term support shows sincerity.
- **Ongoing Mentorship**: If you begin tutoring a younger student, keep supporting them over time, celebrating each milestone.
- **Seasonal Adjustments**: If your schedule changes, adapt your volunteering time but try not to vanish abruptly.

Deep Insight: Long-term service allows you to see real growth in individuals or communities. It also helps you learn perseverance and deeper compassion.

---

16. Creative Ideas for Teens on a Budget

You do not need lots of money to help others. Creativity and willingness can outshine budget limitations.

- **Upcycling**: Transform old materials into blankets or crafts for donation.
- **No-Cost Fundraisers**: Organize a community talent show where attendees can donate items (like canned goods) for entry.
- **Skill Swaps**: Offer lessons in something you are good at—like guitar or painting—and ask participants to donate food items to a local food drive.
- **Community Events**: Plan a free neighborhood clean-up day or a free car wash for seniors. You provide manpower, and the community benefits.

Note: Resourcefulness teaches you that help is not always about money—it is about heart, ideas, and action.

17. Handling Challenges and Discouragement

Service can be tough. You might meet ungrateful people or find that a project fails to meet your expectations. Discouragement is normal, but it should not stop you from continuing.

- **Realistic Expectations**: Understand that not everyone will appreciate your efforts, and some problems might not be fixed overnight.
- **Learn from Failure**: If an event had low turnout, figure out why. Could you have promoted it better? Did you choose a bad time? Adjust and try again.
- **Support System**: Talk to friends, family, or a youth leader when you feel down. They can remind you of the bigger purpose behind your service.
- **Stay Prayerful**: God sees your heart even if results seem small. Ask Him to guide you forward and strengthen your resolve.

Encouragement: Every act of kindness has a ripple effect, even if you do not see the full outcome. Faith reminds you that doing good is valuable, regardless of immediate response.

---

18. Sharing the Message of Christ Through Service

While you help, you also represent Christ. People often pay attention to actions more than words, so your kindness can be a powerful testimony.

- **Let Love Lead**: Showing genuine care draws people's curiosity about your motivation. They might ask, "Why do you bother helping me?" opening a door to share your faith.
- **Avoid Pushing**: Do not force religious conversations. If they ask, share simply about how your faith inspires you. Offer them a chance to learn more, but respect their choice.
- **Pray for Opportunities**: Ask God to place you where someone needs comfort or a listening ear. Sometimes, a quiet but consistent presence can be more impactful than many words.
- **Be Prepared**: If someone has questions about Jesus, know a few Scriptures or personal stories that explain your belief without needing to be an expert.

Powerful Thought: Sometimes, the best way to spread the gospel is by living it out daily. People see Christ in you and become open to exploring faith themselves.

---

19. Building Lasting Friendships

Serving can connect you with people who share your passion for doing good. These friendships often have a deep foundation of shared purpose.

- **Join Local Groups**: Community clubs or volunteer networks can introduce you to classmates or neighbors who are also dedicated to uplifting others.
- **Keep in Touch**: After a project, continue talking to the friends you made. Plan future collaborations.
- **Encourage One Another**: Service can be draining. Friends in the same arena can remind you of the rewards and keep you motivated.
- **Broaden Your View**: Sometimes, you will meet people from different backgrounds. Welcome these differences as a chance to learn.

Insight: Shared service experiences often bond people in a special way. You see each other's compassion, teamwork, and faith in action.

---

20. Moving Forward with a Heart for Service

Helping others is not a one-time choice; it can become a way of life. As you continue, you will learn more about yourself, discover new ways to be useful, and see God's hand at work in small and big ways. This attitude of service shines a light in a world that often focuses on personal gain. Through consistent efforts, you can inspire other teens, bring hope to hurting individuals, and reflect the nature of Jesus, who came "not to be served, but to serve" (Mark 10:45).

Questions for Reflection

1. Which group of people in your community do you feel most drawn to help?

2. What is one practical step you can take this month to serve—alone or with friends?
3. How can you keep a positive attitude when your attempts to help do not go as planned?

Practical Action Point
Choose a service idea—like visiting a nursing home or helping at an animal shelter—and schedule it within the next two weeks. Invite at least one friend or family member to join you. Afterward, write down or discuss what you learned and how it felt to make a difference. If possible, plan a second visit or activity to stay consistent.

Conclusion to Chapter 16
Serving the community is a direct expression of Christian love. Whether you help neighbors, support local organizations, or reach out online, your actions can bring tangible hope to those around you. This service also enriches your faith, teaching lessons of humility, compassion, and perseverance. By looking out for needs, partnering with others, and trusting God's guidance, you will see how one caring effort can spark bigger changes. Step by step, you become an ambassador of kindness, showing that God's love is practical, inclusive, and transformative.

CHAPTER 17

Learning from Role Models

Introduction
Role models can shape how you think, act, and see the world. They can be people in your everyday life—family members, teachers, youth leaders—or individuals you read about in books or watch online. Having good examples can motivate you, give you new ideas, and help you stay focused on positive goals. As a Christian teen girl, you can learn from role models who show kindness, strength, and faith in God.

In this chapter, we will talk about finding and learning from role models in practical ways. You will see how to decide if someone is a healthy influence, how to take lessons from them without losing your own identity, and how to handle disappointments if a role model fails. By the end, you will understand that role models are not perfect but can still be guides that shape you into a confident, faithful young woman.

---

1. Why Role Models Matter

A role model is a person you look up to because of their actions, character, or accomplishments. This person might show qualities you want to develop. Role models matter because:

1. **They Show Possible Paths**: Seeing someone serve God well in their job, family, or community can make you realize you can do it too. They can open your eyes to possibilities you never considered.
2. **They Give Real-Life Examples**: Reading about good values is helpful, but seeing those values lived out is even more powerful. A role model's consistent behavior proves certain virtues are not just theories but choices you can make.
3. **They Provide Guidance**: You can learn from a role model's stories. Hearing how they handled problems can help you avoid mistakes.
4. **They Give Motivation**: When you see someone who overcame obstacles and stayed kind or faithful, it can push you to do the same in your own context.

Reminder: Role models can be close—like a parent or mentor—or distant, such as historical figures, Christian authors, or biblical characters. Each can offer lessons if you approach them thoughtfully.

---

2. Different Kinds of Role Models

Not all role models are the same. You might admire one person's faith, another's leadership, and someone else's creativity. It is okay to learn from multiple people, each showing different strengths. Here are some categories:

1. **Family and Friends**: A faithful grandparent or a caring older sibling can guide you daily. They know you well and can speak truths you need.
2. **Church Leaders**: Pastors, youth leaders, or older believers in your congregation might show you how to love others, teach the Bible, or run outreach programs.
3. **Teachers and Coaches**: They can demonstrate dedication, skill-building, and patience. Some might also model good ethics—like fairness and respect.
4. **Historical or Biblical Figures**: For example, Ruth in the Bible displayed loyalty, Esther showed courage, and Daniel stood firm in convictions. Christian missionaries or reformers might also inspire you with their stories.
5. **Modern Influencers**: Writers, Christian musicians, or public speakers can be role models through their books, interviews, or social media content—if they consistently show good values.

Important Note: You may find some people in your life to be partial role models—you respect their honesty but not their anger problem. That is normal. Take the good while being aware of their flaws.

---

3. Finding Healthy Role Models

You might wonder how to spot a role model worth following. Here are qualities to look for:

- **Consistent Values**: They do not just talk about kindness or integrity; they show it in their actions.
- **Humility**: They admit mistakes and do not act as if they are perfect.
- **Respect for Others**: They treat people of all backgrounds with love and fairness.
- **Growth Mindset**: They keep learning and improving, not stuck in pride or bitterness.
- **Faith in Practice**: If they say they believe in God, you see them praying, studying Scripture, or serving.

Practical Tip: Watch how they handle stress or conflict. Role models who blame others or explode with anger might not be ideal. Look for someone who remains calm, seeks solutions, and stays respectful under pressure.

---

4. Learning from Mentors or Spiritual Leaders

Sometimes, you can have a direct relationship with a mentor—someone who invests time to help you grow. This can happen through a youth program, a church small group, or a natural friendship that develops.

- **Asking for Guidance**: If you see a church member whose faith you admire, ask if you can have short meetups to talk or pray together. This can be once a month over coffee or a weekly chat after church.
- **Listening Actively**: When they share experiences, take notes or remember key points. Apply these lessons in your life, even if it feels small at first.
- **Asking Questions**: Be honest about your doubts, personal challenges, or confusions about faith. A mentor can share insights from their own walk with God.
- **Being Respectful of Their Time**: Mentors are often busy. Be punctual and prepared for your meetups, and express gratitude for their help.

Rare Insight: A mentor-mentee relationship works best when both sides communicate clearly. If something is not working or you feel you need different guidance, discuss it kindly.

---

5. Using the Bible as a Source of Role Models

Scripture contains stories of many individuals who walked with God. You can study their lives for examples, warnings, and encouragement.

- **Reading with Purpose**: Instead of just reading a random chapter, pick a Bible character who interests you—like Mary, David, Joseph, or Paul. Read their story carefully.
- **Observing Strengths**: Joseph's perseverance, for instance, can teach you patience. Ruth's loyalty can show you steadfast friendship.
- **Noting Weaknesses**: Many biblical figures had flaws. David sinned, Jonah ran from God, Peter denied Jesus. Seeing how God still worked through them can remind you that mistakes do not disqualify you from God's plan.
- **Applying Lessons**: If you admire Daniel's courage in worship, think about ways you can stay true to your faith in a challenging environment—like at school or in peer pressure situations.

Deep Thought: The Bible never hides the struggles of its main characters, which shows that real people, not superhumans, can demonstrate faith. This encourages you to aim for growth, not perfection.

---

6. Drawing Lessons from Historical or Modern Christian Figures

Reading Christian biographies or testimonies can open your eyes to real-life stories of faith. This might include missionaries who traveled far to share the gospel, activists who fought for justice, or everyday believers who changed lives in small towns.

- **Real Examples of Perseverance**: These figures often faced hardships—like illness, lack of funds, or opposition—but they kept relying on God.
- **Practical Strategies**: They might share how they balanced prayer, service, and personal rest. You can adapt their methods to your own life.
- **Inspiration for Your Calling**: Hearing how someone discovered their purpose can help you reflect on your own gifts and direction.
- **Insight into God's Work Globally**: Sometimes, reading about a missionary in another country helps you see that God is active everywhere, not just in your local area.

Rare Benefit: Some of these figures wrote journals or diaries that you can read. Seeing their honest struggles can remind you that doubt or fatigue is normal, and leaning on God can bring renewed energy.

---

7. Learning from Non-Christian Role Models (With Caution)

You might admire certain musicians, authors, athletes, or entrepreneurs who are not Christians. They can have strong work ethic, creativity, or leadership skills. It is possible to learn from them, but be mindful about adopting their worldview.

- **Separate Skills from Values**: You can appreciate their discipline or artistry without imitating any lifestyle choices that clash with biblical teachings.
- **Maintain Discernment**: If their content strongly contradicts God's truths or promotes harmful behaviors, consider limiting how much you expose yourself to it.
- **Pick Out the Good**: Maybe an athlete's dedication to training or an artist's creative process can still teach you persistence.
- **Stay Grounded in Faith**: Keep a firm base in your beliefs. If a non-Christian role model's message conflicts with biblical wisdom, do not compromise your convictions.

Practical Example: You might watch a famous athlete's documentary for tips on discipline, but if they also promote selfish or destructive attitudes, you skip that part and focus only on their beneficial training methods.

---

8. Avoiding Idolizing Your Role Models

It is easy to look at someone's highlight reel and think they must be perfect, forgetting they are human. Idolizing a person can lead to disappointment or misguided loyalty.

- **Stay Aware of Flaws**: Even the best role model has weaknesses. If you ignore that, you might copy their negative traits too.

- **Remember God Above All**: Ultimately, you follow Christ. People can fail you, but God remains your perfect guide.
- **Watch for Unhealthy Obsession**: If you find yourself trying to be exactly like a role model in every way—dressing the same, talking the same—take a step back. Keep your own identity.
- **Be Open to Many Examples**: Do not rely on just one person's voice. Listening to different viewpoints can help you stay balanced.

Deep Reminder: While a role model can point you to good habits, only God deserves your ultimate devotion. People might reflect a piece of God's character, but they are not God Himself.

9. Taking Specific Notes and Actions

Learning from a role model is more effective if you move beyond just admiring them. Write down or remember key lessons and put them into practice.

- **Keep a Role Model Journal**: Dedicate a small notebook or a digital note to record quotes, actions, or teachings you find inspiring.
- **Set Small Goals**: For instance, if you admire your aunt's kindness, pick one day a week to practice a thoughtful act, like calling a lonely friend or sending a note.
- **Reflect on Results**: After applying a lesson, check how it affected your life or mood. Did it draw you closer to God, improve relationships, or give you more peace?
- **Stay Flexible**: You might try a role model's habit but find it does not fit your personality. That is fine. Adjust and try what works for you.

Encouragement: Turning lessons into real actions is the difference between daydreaming and true growth. God can use your efforts to shape your character and bless those around you.

10. Handling Disappointment if a Role Model Fails

It can be shocking when someone you admire does something morally wrong or publicly stumbles. You might feel betrayed or lose faith in what they taught. Here's how to handle it:

1. **Acknowledge the Pain**: It is normal to feel upset, angry, or confused. Share these emotions with God or a trusted friend.
2. **Separate Their Actions from Their Lessons**: If they taught biblical truths that you know are correct, those truths remain valid even if the teacher failed to follow them.
3. **Remember Human Frailty**: Everyone struggles with sin. This does not excuse wrongdoing but reminds you that no person is beyond failing.
4. **Seek Wise Counsel**: Talk to another mentor or pastor about your disappointment. They can help you process it.
5. **Decide Your Ongoing Response**: You may still learn from some parts of their example while rejecting behaviors that hurt you or others. Or you may choose to remove their influence from your life if the fall was severe and unrepentant.

Hopeful Thought: A role model's failure can remind you to always keep your primary trust in God. People can reflect goodness, but they are not the source of goodness.

---

11. Supporting Younger People as a Role Model Yourself

Being a role model is not just for adults. You can be a guiding example for those younger than you—even for friends your own age—by living out your faith and integrity.

- **Be Consistent**: Younger students or siblings watch how you act at home, at church, and online. If you say one thing but do another, they will notice.
- **Share Encouragement**: Offer kindness, help them with homework, or invite them to positive activities. Even small acts can shape how they view older teens.
- **Admit Imperfections**: You do not have to pretend to be flawless. If you make a mistake, apologize and move forward. This shows them honesty and humility.
- **Pray for Them**: Ask God to give you wisdom in guiding them. You might also pray for them to grow in faith and character.

Special Note: Realize that some kids or peers might look up to you even if you do not know it. Maintaining good choices can quietly influence them to follow suit.

12. Watching Out for Online Role Models

In a digital age, you may follow Christian speakers on social media, watch YouTube sermons, or read blogs from influential people. Some might become virtual role models.

- **Examine Their Fruit**: Do they show real faith-based content that points to Jesus, or is it more about personal fame? Watch for patterns in how they talk, how they treat others, and how they handle critics.
- **Check Their Sources**: A popular figure might share questionable theology if they twist Scripture. Ensure they align with core Christian teachings.
- **Avoid Blind Devotion**: If you disagree on a vital point, do not ignore it just because they have a large following. You can appreciate parts of their message but stay loyal to God's Word first.
- **Mind Your Time**: Spending too much time on any influencer's feed can distract from personal Bible reading or face-to-face fellowship. Keep balance.

Practical Suggestion: If an online mentor promotes moral or biblical values that differ from your church's understanding, ask a pastor or a knowledgeable friend for perspective. Compare what they teach with the Bible.

---

13. Blending Different Role Models for a Full Picture

Instead of focusing on one person, gather lessons from various role models. This way, you develop a well-rounded perspective.

- **Mix Different Strengths**: One role model might show you how to be a good listener, another shows strong leadership, and another shows deep kindness.
- **Avoid Comparison Stress**: If you only look at one extremely talented person, you might feel you can never measure up. By learning from many, you realize each quality can grow in small steps.
- **Consider Different Age Groups**: Some role models can be peers who show devotion to God, while others can be older individuals with life experience. Both can be valuable.

- **Update as You Grow**: As you mature, you might find new role models who fit your stage in life. Keep an open mind while staying faithful to biblical truths.

Encouragement: Gathering good traits from several people can form a stronger character foundation. You do not have to be exactly like any one person to succeed.

---

14. Reflecting on Role Model Influence in Your Life

It is helpful to step back and notice how role models affect you. Sometimes, you might pick up good or bad habits without realizing it.

- **Check Your Behavior**: Are you repeating phrases or copying styles from someone? Is this beneficial or harmful?
- **Compare to Scripture**: If your new habits clash with God's commands (like being proud or disrespectful), it is time to adjust.
- **Write Down Changes**: Make a brief list of ways you have grown because of a mentor or admired figure—maybe you pray more, study more, or speak more kindly. This boosts your gratitude and awareness.
- **Stay Watchful**: If a role model starts promoting questionable ideas, you need to reevaluate how much you follow them. People change, and so can their advice.

Practical Action: Every few months, do a quick check-up on your influences. Ask God to show you if you are drifting in any area. This keeps your growth on track.

---

15. Standing on Your Own Identity

While role models help shape you, you still must be yourself—unique and designed by God for a special purpose. Copying someone else's personality or calling might lead to frustration.

- **Know Your Gifts**: If you admire a singer but your gift is teaching kids, do not force yourself to sing just because your role model does. Take the lessons about passion or discipline but apply them to your own calling.

- **Protect Your Conscience**: If your role model does something you feel uneasy about, trust your convictions. You do not have to follow them there.
- **Embrace Your Limits**: Some role models are extremely outgoing or physically strong. If that is not you, do not feel like you are less. You have talents that fit you best.
- **Be True to God's Leading**: In prayer, ask God for direction. He might use a role model to hint at a path, but He speaks to you directly too, through His Word and the Holy Spirit.

Encouragement: God did not create clones. He uses each person's personality for unique tasks. Learn from others but remain genuine to how God formed you.

16. Sharing With Friends About Good Role Models

When you find a helpful role model—maybe a speaker, a book, or a youth leader—tell your friends about them. You can grow together.

- **Recommend Resources**: If you read an inspiring Christian biography, pass it on. If you found a preacher whose messages speak truth, share a link.
- **Group Discussions**: Invite friends to watch a sermon or read a chapter of a role model's book. Then chat about it. Hearing diverse viewpoints can expand your learning.
- **Accountability**: If a group of you want to apply the same lessons, you can keep each other accountable and talk about your progress or challenges.
- **Watch for Varied Preferences**: Not everyone resonates with the same role model. That is okay. Suggest options but let them choose what suits their interests and spiritual growth.

Deep Benefit: Role models can shape an entire circle of friends. When many are influenced by a wise, godly example, your group can become more united and positive.

17. Knowing When to Step Away from a Role Model

Sometimes, a role model changes direction or starts promoting ideas that conflict with biblical truths. You might also see behaviors that show they are no longer a trustworthy example.

- **Red Flags**: If they encourage hate, pride, or actions that go against Scripture. If they lie or manipulate others often.
- **Confusion**: If you keep feeling uneasy or noticing a clash between their outward persona and real conduct.
- **Seek Counsel**: Talk to a parent or church leader about your concerns. They might confirm your observations or offer a different viewpoint.
- **Gracious Exit**: You do not have to announce it publicly. You can quietly reduce or stop following their content or teachings.

Calming Thought: It is not disloyal to walk away if a role model's life no longer aligns with God's ways. Staying faithful to God is always the priority.

---

18. Praying for Your Role Models

Even if someone is strong in faith, they need prayers. Leading and influencing others can bring bigger trials or temptations for them.

- **Regular Intercession**: Lift them up in prayer, asking God to protect them, grant them wisdom, and keep their motives pure.
- **Pray for Growth**: Role models also continue to learn. Pray they remain humble and open to correction.
- **Pray for Their Families**: If they are public figures, their loved ones also face pressure. Interceding can protect them from stress or division.
- **Pray for Their Impact**: Ask God to use their platform to reach people with truth. Pray that those who listen to them will be led to know Jesus more deeply.

Note: Praying for your role models reminds you they are human, reliant on God just like you. It also keeps your heart soft and supportive.

19. Combining Role Model Lessons with Scripture

In everything, Scripture remains the highest authority. You might gather wisdom from role models, but always compare it to God's Word to ensure it lines up with truth.

- **Check Teachings**: If a teacher says something about relationships or morality, confirm that it aligns with biblical guidelines, such as those found in Romans, Ephesians, or the Gospels.
- **Look for Fruit**: The Bible says you will know someone by their fruit (Matthew 7:16). Fruit means their actions and how they affect others. If it is consistent with love, joy, peace, patience, kindness, goodness, faithfulness, gentleness, and self-control, it is likely good fruit.
- **Stay in Prayer**: Ask God to show you if a role model's advice fits His Word. The Holy Spirit can nudge your heart if something is off.

Lifelong Practice: This habit of testing teachings or actions by Scripture will protect you from confusion and keep you rooted in genuine faith.

---

20. Moving Forward with Confidence and Care

Learning from role models is a powerful way to shape your future. As you keep your eyes on God, glean wisdom from people who reflect His love and truth. Take the best lessons and weave them into your life, but remember you have a unique calling that cannot be replaced by anyone else's path. By staying humble, prayerful, and open to growth, you will keep learning from those who go before you and pass on good examples to those who come after.

Questions for Reflection

1. Which type of role model do you connect with the most—family, historical/biblical, modern Christian figures, or others? Why?
2. How can you apply one lesson from a favorite role model in your life this week?
3. Do you have any role model you need to rethink because of conflicts with biblical truth?

Practical Action Point
Pick one role model—maybe a church mentor, a biblical character, or a Christian leader you follow online. Write down three qualities you admire about them and how you see those qualities in action. Then make a simple plan for how you can start building one of those qualities in your daily life. For example, if you admire their prayer life, decide on a specific time and place each day for your own prayer routine. Monitor your progress for at least a week, noting any changes in your mindset or habits.

Conclusion to Chapter 17
Role models are guides who show you what is possible when someone chooses faith, integrity, and compassion. You do not have to copy them blindly. Instead, look for consistent values, compare their actions with Scripture, and gather specific lessons that can help you form your own godly lifestyle. When disappointment arises, keep your focus on God, who never fails. By learning from role models but keeping Christ as your ultimate example, you will grow stronger in faith, character, and purpose.

CHAPTER 18

Setting Goals with Faith

Introduction
Goals shape your direction in life. They are like road signs that point you toward what you hope to achieve, whether it is improving your grades, building stronger friendships, or deepening your walk with God. As a Christian teen girl, your goals can reflect both your personal passions and the values taught in Scripture. When you align your dreams with God's wisdom, you gain a sense of purpose that goes beyond simple success.

In this chapter, we will talk about how to set meaningful goals that incorporate faith. You will learn why goal-setting matters, how to create realistic action steps, and how to keep going when obstacles appear. We will also cover ways to involve prayer and biblical principles in every stage of planning. By the end, you will see that goals guided by faith are not restrictive—they can help you become more effective, balanced, and spiritually grounded.

1. Why Goals Matter for a Christian Teen

Setting goals is not just for adults. You might have short-term goals, like finishing a school project, or long-term goals, like choosing a future career path. Goals matter because:

1. **They Bring Clarity**: Goals help you recognize what is important. This clarity can protect you from drifting or wasting time.
2. **They Create Motivation**: Having a clear target gives you energy to push through challenges.
3. **They Teach Responsibility**: Reaching a goal often requires discipline, problem-solving, and wise use of resources—skills that will serve you your entire life.
4. **They Help You Live Out Faith**: When you set faith-based goals, you practice surrendering your plans to God's will, learning to trust Him with the outcomes.

Encouragement: Goals do not have to be huge or life-changing. Even a small aim, like spending 10 minutes in daily prayer, can yield profound growth over time.

2. Aligning Goals with Biblical Principles

As you think about what you want to achieve, it is crucial to see if your goals fit with God's Word. This step ensures you do not chase things that harm you or move you away from faith.

- **Check Your Motives**: Ask yourself why you want this goal. Is it to honor God, help others, or grow personally, or is it purely for pride or selfish desires?
- **Look for Scripture Support**: For instance, if your goal is to manage stress, the Bible supports the idea of seeking peace through prayer (Philippians 4:6-7). If your goal is to improve relationships, Scripture emphasizes love and forgiveness.
- **Ask for Spiritual Guidance**: Pray, asking God to show you if a goal aligns with His plan. Sometimes, He may redirect you to a different path.
- **Consider the Fruit**: Will achieving this goal produce good outcomes—like joy, kindness, service? Or could it lead to envy, harm, or neglect of your spiritual life?

Practical Check: Before you finalize a goal, write down the reasons you believe it honors God. This list can motivate you when your drive fades or distractions come.

---

3. Examples of Faith-Focused Goals

Not every goal must mention "God" to be faith-based. Any goal that aims for good, respects biblical values, and serves others can reflect your faith. Some examples:

1. **Spiritual Growth**: Reading a chapter of the Bible daily, joining a small group, or memorizing Scripture each week.
2. **Character Development**: Improving patience, controlling anger, or practicing daily gratitude.
3. **Academic Efforts**: Working diligently in school, using your knowledge to honor God and serve others.
4. **Service Goals**: Volunteering at a shelter for a set number of hours each month, organizing a church drive for those in need.

5. **Health and Well-Being**: Exercising regularly and caring for your body as a temple of the Holy Spirit (1 Corinthians 6:19-20).

Deep Insight: A faith-based goal is not limited to church activities. Even a goal to improve your time management can be faith-based if it allows you to serve more effectively or maintain a peaceful mindset for prayer.

---

4. Using the S.M.A.R.T. Approach

A common tool for goal setting is to make them S.M.A.R.T.:

- **Specific**: Clearly define what you want. Example: "I want to read the entire Gospel of John in one month."
- **Measurable**: Decide how to track progress. For the reading goal, you could read one chapter a day, so you know if you are on schedule.
- **Achievable**: Set goals within reach but still challenging. Reading one chapter a day is manageable. Trying to read 20 chapters daily might be too much.
- **Realistic**: Consider your actual schedule and responsibilities. If you have major exams, be practical about how much time you can devote.
- **Time-Bound**: Give a target date or timeframe. A month to finish reading John gives you a clear end point.

Faith Twist: In each step, keep God at the center. Ask, "Is this goal something I sense God approving? Does it fit my calling, or am I forcing it?"

---

5. Breaking Down Big Goals into Steps

Large goals—like deciding on a future career or reading the entire Bible—can seem overwhelming. Splitting them into smaller tasks can build momentum.

- **Divide into Phases**: For example, reading the entire Bible might be broken down into reading one to two chapters a day, finishing one book at a time.
- **Recognize Small Milestones**: After finishing a book of the Bible or a month of consistent study, pause to note your achievement . This encourages you to keep going.

- **Track Daily or Weekly**: Keep a planner or checklist. Seeing boxes checked off can fuel motivation.
- **Stay Flexible**: If something changes—like you get sick or have extra responsibilities—adjust your plan. Rescheduling is better than giving up.

Practical Example: If your big goal is to improve your math grade by the end of the semester, smaller steps might include studying 20 minutes daily, attending a weekly tutoring session, and doing extra practice problems on weekends. Each step leads you closer to the larger achievement.

---

6. Seeking God's Will in Your Plans

A Christian approach to goal-setting involves more than just picking tasks. You want to align with God's will, trusting He knows what is best for you. This mindset can reduce anxiety since you know your future is in capable hands.

- **Regular Prayer**: Pray about your goals from the start, not after you decide everything. Ask for wisdom, direction, and the right heart posture.
- **Listen for Guidance**: Sometimes, a verse might stand out, or a sermon might address your situation, confirming or reshaping your plans.
- **Be Open to Change**: You might set a goal for a certain college but sense God leading you elsewhere. Being flexible allows you to follow His better plan.
- **Trust God's Timing**: If progress is slower than you want, do not assume failure. God might be teaching patience or preparing you in ways you cannot see.

Biblical Support: Proverbs 3:5-6 encourages us to trust in the Lord with all our heart and lean not on our own understanding, promising He will direct our paths.

7. Writing Down Your Goals and Prayers

Putting your goals on paper (or in a digital note) makes them more concrete. You can also add related Bible verses or prayer points. Some helpful tips:

- **Goal Journal**: Dedicate a small notebook to list each goal, why it matters, the steps you plan, and any deadlines.
- **Prayer List**: Next to each goal, note how you will pray for God's help. For example, "Goal: Improve communication with my mom. Prayer: Ask God for patience and calm words."
- **Review Regularly**: Glance over your journal weekly to see what needs attention.
- **Record God's Answers**: When you see progress or an unexpected blessing, jot it down. This will remind you of God's involvement.

Deep Benefit: This practice not only organizes your tasks but also strengthens your faith as you see tangible answers and growth over time.

---

8. Balancing Spiritual Goals with Everyday Duties

Being a teenager often means juggling many responsibilities—school, home chores, extracurriculars. It is important to make sure your spiritual goals fit into your real-world schedule.

- **Set Realistic Expectations**: If you have hours of homework each night, aiming for two hours of prayer daily might be unrealistic. Instead, you could break your prayer time into 10-minute segments.
- **Attach Spiritual Habits to Existing Routines**: You could pray for five minutes before bed or read a devotional during breakfast. This makes it easier to remember.
- **Use Idle Moments**: Pray on the bus, listen to Christian podcasts while doing chores, or memorize Scripture verses during short study breaks.
- **Stay True to Commitments**: Achieving academic success or helping your family can also be ways of honoring God, so do not neglect them for the sake of extra spiritual projects. Balance matters.

Encouragement: God is present in every part of your day, not just in formal "religious" times. Inviting Him into your normal tasks can make them part of your faith journey.

9. Dealing with Distractions and Time-Wasters

Even the best plans can fail if you lose hours to aimless social media scrolling or other distractions. Setting boundaries helps keep you focused on your goals.

- **Identify Your Main Distractions**: It could be a certain app, endless texting, or binge-watching shows.
- **Use Timers or Limits**: Many phones allow app limits. If you go beyond an hour, the app locks automatically.
- **Reward System**: Complete your study goal, then allow yourself 15 minutes of a fun show. Keep it moderate.
- **Accountability Buddy**: Team up with a friend who also wants to manage distractions. You can check each other's progress.

Thought: Recognize that your time is a gift from God. Wasting large chunks of it can rob you of chances to grow, serve, or rest properly.

---

10. Encouraging Yourself with God's Promises

When working toward a goal, discouragement might creep in. Perhaps you do not see quick progress, or you face setbacks. Biblical promises can lift your spirit:

- **God's Presence**: Joshua 1:9 reminds you to be strong and courageous because God is with you. This can comfort you if you feel alone in your pursuits.
- **God's Strength in Weakness**: 2 Corinthians 12:9 says that God's power is shown in our weakness. This means you do not have to be perfect.
- **Hope and Future**: Jeremiah 29:11 speaks of the good plans God has for His people. While context matters, it still shows God's care for your future.
- **Perseverance**: Galatians 6:9 urges you not to grow tired of doing good, for in due time, you will reap a reward if you do not give up.

Practical Action: Memorize one verse that resonates with your current goal. Repeat it when you feel like quitting.

11. Handling Peer Pressure About Your Goals

Sometimes, friends do not understand why you are prioritizing certain goals—like spending more time on church activities or cutting back on social media to study. They may tease you or say you are "too serious."

- **Explain Briefly**: You can say, "I'm focusing on improving my grades," or "I want to grow in my faith." You do not have to give a long sermon—just a calm statement of why this matters.
- **Stay Confident**: If you are sure this aligns with God's plan, do not let opinions pull you off track. Respect their views, but continue your path.
- **Find Supportive Friends**: Spend more time with those who respect your aspirations. Seek people who also aim for personal growth.
- **Set Boundaries**: If certain people constantly mock you, limit how much personal information you share about your goals. Keep your circle of trust small.

Deep Reminder: Peer pressure can be strong, but God's guidance is stronger. Standing firm can also quietly encourage others to reflect on their own priorities.

---

12. Celebrating Progress and Growth

Reaching a milestone is worth noting. This does not mean bragging; it is about thanking God and staying encouraged.

- **Mark Mini-Milestones**: If your goal is to read the Bible in a year, mark each completed book with a small note in your planner.
- **Prayer of Gratitude**: When you hit a goal, pray, thanking God for strength. This keeps the focus on His help.
- **Share Good News with Mentors**: If a youth leader or parent supported you, let them know you reached your milestone. Their feedback can boost your hope.
- **Reflect on Lessons**: What did you learn about discipline, faith, or humility along the way? Summarize these insights in your journal.

Caution: Watch out for pride. Marking achievements should point back to God's goodness, not inflate your ego.

13. Learning from Mistakes or Delays

Goals rarely unfold perfectly. You might encounter failures—like missing a deadline or slipping into old habits. Instead of giving up, see these moments as growth points.

- **Admit the Setback**: Pretending it did not happen hinders you from learning. Acknowledge the misstep.
- **Analyze the Cause**: Were you too ambitious? Did you procrastinate? Did you ignore potential warning signs?
- **Adapt Your Plan**: Adjust timelines or break the goal into more steps if it felt too large.
- **Seek Encouragement**: Talk to a mentor or friend. Sometimes a little reassurance helps you get back on track.
- **Focus Forward**: Dwelling on failure can trap you. Accept that mistakes happen, and keep moving toward your goal with fresh determination.

Reassurance: Mistakes do not erase your progress. They can actually refine your approach. God can use setbacks to teach dependence on Him and develop resilience.

---

14. Combining Group and Personal Goals

Some goals are private—like improving personal prayer habits. Others might be group-centered—like forming a choir or a prayer circle at school. Balancing both can help you grow socially and spiritually.

- **Personal Goals**: These might involve private devotions, personal character changes, or specific tasks only you handle. Keep these in your daily routine.
- **Group Goals**: You might gather friends to run a Bible study or host a fundraiser for a cause. This requires coordination, shared responsibilities, and open communication.
- **Mutual Accountability**: In group goals, you hold each other to the tasks. If one person slacks, it affects everyone, which can push you to be reliable.
- **Learning Teamwork**: You might not always agree on the best approach. This is a chance to practice patience and respect as you work together toward a common aim.

Practical Example: You could have a personal goal to memorize a Psalm each week and a group goal where you and your friends clean up a local park monthly. Each type of goal develops different skills and virtues.

---

15. Handling Shifts in Goals Over Time

Your interests, responsibilities, and life circumstances change. A goal that was crucial last year might not fit this year. Be open to adapting or even replacing goals as you grow.

- **Regular Goal Check**: Every few months, review your list. Are you still passionate about them? Have new opportunities emerged?
- **Pray for Renewal**: Ask God if you should keep pushing or if He is guiding you to a new focus.
- **Avoid Shame**: Changing a goal or letting one go does not mean failure. Sometimes, it is a sign of growth or new direction.
- **Celebrate (Use "Recognize") Achievements**: Even if you do not fully complete a goal, you might have learned valuable lessons. Mark that progress before moving on.

Key Insight: Life is dynamic, and so is your journey of faith. Adjusting goals can help you keep pace with how God is working in your heart and environment.

---

16. Incorporating Service into Your Goals

Your goals do not have to be self-centered. Consider adding a service angle. For instance, if your goal is to get better at art, you could plan to create greeting cards for a nursing home. Or if you want to learn new recipes, you might cook meals for a local shelter once a month.

- **Link Personal Growth to Helping Others**: This transforms your efforts into a blessing.
- **Motivation to Keep Going**: Knowing your progress helps someone else can inspire you when you feel lazy or doubtful.
- **Build Compassion**: As you develop your skills, you remain aware of other people's needs, preventing selfishness.

- **Showcase Christian Love**: Service-based goals demonstrate practical faith to those around you.

Deep Reward: Serving through your goals can expand your perspective. You might discover deeper joy and purpose in something you initially pursued just for yourself.

---

17. Using Technology Wisely for Goal Tracking

Technology can support your efforts if used carefully. Here are some ways to leverage digital tools without letting them take over:

- **Goal-Tracking Apps**: Some apps let you set daily habits, track streaks, and send reminders. They can be especially helpful for tasks like reading the Bible, practicing an instrument, or journaling.
- **Online Accountability**: You could join a faith-based group chat where members share daily progress on certain goals. Encouragement from like-minded peers can boost your morale.
- **Digital Planners**: A simple calendar app can map out your entire month, marking key dates for each milestone.
- **Alerts and Alarms**: If you plan to pray at a certain time, set a gentle alarm to pause whatever you are doing. Just ensure you do not click "dismiss" and ignore it every time.

Caution: Keep an eye on how much time you spend managing your goals digitally vs. actually working on them. Also, guard against the urge to share everything on social media just for likes or approval.

---

18. Praying Over Each Step

Inviting God into every step keeps your focus on Him rather than just the end result. Prayer reminds you that achievements are not purely your doing but also come from His grace.

- **Start with Prayer**: Before you begin a new goal, pray for wisdom to plan effectively and a humble heart.

- **Pray Through Obstacles**: When you hit a hard spot, pause and ask God for guidance instead of panicking.
- **Thanksgiving**: After small wins, pause to thank God. This nurtures gratitude and prevents pride.
- **Pray for Impact**: If your goal has a service aspect, ask God to use your efforts to bless others, even if you never see the full impact.

Reassurance: James 1:5 says if you lack wisdom, you can ask God, who gives generously. This promise covers every aspect of life, including your personal goals.

19. Encouraging Friends to Set Faith-Based Goals

As you benefit from solid goals, you can also motivate friends. A supportive environment multiplies positive change.

- **Offer to Plan Together**: Have a small gathering or online meet where each person shares a goal and how it ties to faith.
- **Support Each Other**: Ask about progress, pray together, and swap tips. This accountability can help everyone stay on track.
- **Respect Differences**: Your friends might focus on different areas—like one on health, another on mission work, another on improving family relationships. Cheer them on, even if your paths differ.
- **Share Resources**: If you find a good devotional or a helpful app, let your friends know. They might return the favor.

Larger Vision: A circle of friends committed to God-honoring goals can transform your youth group or school environment. Others might see the positive energy and want to join.

20. Conclusion: Walking Forward with Hope

Setting goals as a Christian teen girl is not about adding pressure or seeking worldly trophies. It is about stewarding your talents, time, and purpose in line with God's call. When you allow faith to guide your aims, your daily tasks gain deeper meaning. Each step—whether big or small—can help you become more faithful, loving, and effective in the world around you. Even if challenges arise, you can stand firm, knowing God supports you and that each milestone can help you shine His light more brightly.

Questions for Reflection

1. What is one faith-based goal you have been thinking about, and what first step can you take right now?
2. How can you handle distractions or peer pressures that might sidetrack you from this goal?
3. Which Bible verse can you memorize to encourage you when you feel stuck?

Practical Action Point
Select one goal—big or small—and apply the S.M.A.R.T. method (with faith in mind). Write it down in detail. Then share it with a friend or mentor, asking them to pray for you. At the end of the first week, review how it went, noting any progress or roadblocks. Make small adjustments if necessary and keep praying for wisdom.

Summary of Chapters 17 and 18

- **Chapter 17** focused on learning from role models. It explained how to find positive examples, whether they are family members, biblical figures, or modern Christians. You learned how to filter out unhealthy influences, avoid putting anyone on a pedestal, and even become a role model for those younger than you.
- **Chapter 18** discussed setting goals with faith at the center. It covered why goals matter, how to align them with God's Word, and methods to plan realistically. You saw ways to weave prayer into every step, handle setbacks, and stay true to your call even when peers do not understand.

By combining these lessons, you can follow solid role models who guide you to good habits while laying out clear goals that honor God and shape your future. Both chapters emphasize practical steps—taking notes, using S.M.A.R.T. guidelines, and staying connected to Scripture and prayer. You are now better equipped to grow in faith, character, and purpose, with confidence that God is with you on every step of the path.

CHAPTER 19

Building a Bright Future

Introduction

When you are a teenager, thinking about the future can feel both exciting and scary. Questions might swirl around where to go for higher education, what career path to choose, or how to handle finances later on. Even smaller decisions—like which subjects to focus on or what extracurriculars to pursue—can seem enormous. As a Christian teen girl, you have the advantage of seeking God's wisdom in your planning. This chapter will guide you in how to prepare for a bright future without being overwhelmed. You will see how faith shapes not only your goals, but also your approach to decision-making, relationships, and responsibilities.

We will talk about practical steps to become more independent, how to manage your resources, and ways to keep trusting God's plan even when the path looks uncertain. You will also learn how small habits formed now can lead to big payoffs in adulthood. By combining biblical principles with practical insights, you can step into the years ahead with confidence, knowing that God cares about every aspect of your growth.

---

1. Embracing Responsibility

As you grow older, more opportunities and responsibilities come your way. Handling them well sets a strong foundation for the future.

- **Ownership of Tasks**: Instead of waiting for reminders from parents or teachers, take initiative. If you notice chores piling up at home or group assignments at school, start organizing solutions.
- **Time Management**: Learn to schedule your day. Include school, homework, hobbies, devotions, and some downtime. A balanced approach prevents stress and shows you can handle multiple areas of life.
- **Financial Basics**: Even if you only have a small allowance or a part-time job, start learning to budget. Practice saving a portion, giving to church or charity, and using the rest wisely.

- **Healthy Boundaries**: Decide how much time you will devote to certain activities or friendships. Setting these limits protects your energy and helps you follow your values.

Faith Angle: The Bible encourages diligence and responsibility (Colossians 3:23). By willingly taking on tasks, you not only honor God but also develop essential life skills.

---

2. Exploring Career or Education Paths

Although you might not have to choose a career immediately, thinking ahead can reduce confusion later. God has given you gifts and interests that can point you toward certain fields.

- **Identify Passions**: What subjects do you naturally enjoy? Which activities feel rewarding? Reflecting on these questions can hint at areas you might explore further.
- **Research Options**: Look into various careers or college majors that match your interests. Check what kind of training or degrees they require.
- **Talk to People in the Field**: If you are curious about nursing, for instance, ask a nurse at church about her experiences. If you are drawn to teaching, speak to a teacher you respect.
- **Job Shadow or Intern**: Some schools or community programs offer short internships or shadow days. These can give you a taste of real-world work.

Spiritual Perspective: Ask God to guide your steps. James 1:5 reminds you that He gives wisdom to those who ask. This might lead you to notice certain talents or open doors to unexpected paths.

---

3. Developing Practical Life Skills

The future is not just about career success; it involves day-to-day responsibilities that can feel daunting if you have never practiced them. Learning these skills now reduces stress later.

- **Basic Cooking**: Know how to cook a few healthy meals. This saves money and improves your health. Look up simple recipes or ask a parent or mentor to show you.
- **Household Tasks**: From laundry to basic cleaning, these chores will keep your living space orderly. Cultivating consistency helps you avoid overwhelm.
- **Simple Repairs**: Understand how to change a light bulb, check smoke detector batteries, or tighten a loose screw. Little fixes keep your environment safe and functional.
- **Transportation**: If you plan to drive, study your state's driver's manual thoroughly. If you use public transportation, learn to read schedules and plan routes.

Faith Connection: Taking care of everyday tasks reflects good stewardship of what God has entrusted to you (Luke 16:10). By handling small matters responsibly, you show readiness for larger opportunities.

---

4. Managing Money Wisely

Money issues can cause stress if you are not equipped. Building good financial habits now can spare you major headaches later.

- **Budget Basics**: Note your income (allowance, gift money, small job earnings) and track expenses (snacks, clothing, phone bill, etc.). Even if the numbers are small, the discipline matters.
- **Saving Goals**: Decide on a percentage you want to save each time you get money. This fosters discipline and builds an emergency fund or future college fund.
- **Giving**: The Bible teaches generosity. Even if you have little, setting aside a portion to give fosters a heart of kindness.
- **Avoiding Debt**: As you age, you might be offered credit cards or loans. Understand interest rates and only borrow what you can repay. If you learn to avoid unnecessary debt, you keep financial freedom.

Encouragement: Scripture often warns against reckless borrowing (Proverbs 22:7). Learning to live within your means frees you from undue stress and aligns with biblical principles.

5. Strengthening Personal Values

Your values guide daily decisions—how you speak, how you treat others, and how you choose friends or handle temptations. Clarifying them now sets a moral compass for the future.

- **Identify Core Beliefs**: Write down what you stand for: honesty, respect, faith, purity, kindness, etc. This list becomes a reference when you face tricky choices.
- **Avoiding Compromise**: If you know cheating goes against your integrity, you will not do it to get ahead. Standing by your values builds trust in yourself and from others.
- **Setting Boundaries**: Values help you draw lines. If you value purity, you will limit certain media or set rules in dating. If you value generosity, you will look for ways to give, not just receive.
- **Review Regularly**: As you grow, you might refine or expand your values. Checking them from time to time ensures they remain strong.

Example: Daniel in the Bible resolved not to defile himself with the king's food (Daniel 1). His unwavering stance, formed early, guided him through future challenges. Likewise, clarity in your values can keep you on track.

---

6. Building Supportive Relationships

A bright future often involves good connections—friends, mentors, and family who encourage your growth. Surrounding yourself with people who respect your faith and ambitions makes a big difference.

- **Seek Positive Influences**: Identify peers or older mentors who share or support your Christian principles. Spend time with them, learn from their experiences, and maintain uplifting conversations.
- **Limit Negative Relationships**: If certain groups push you toward gossip, dishonesty, or disrespect, reduce your time with them. You can be polite but firm about your boundaries.
- **Value Diverse Perspectives**: You can learn from people of different backgrounds or ages. They might offer wisdom you have not considered.

- **Communicate Openly**: If you sense a friendship drifting, talk about it calmly. Avoid silent resentments. Genuine communication can mend misunderstandings.

Biblical Context: Proverbs 13:20 says, "Walk with the wise and become wise." Choosing friends and mentors who uplift you spiritually and morally enhances your outlook on life.

---

7. Handling Stress and Anxiety About the Future

Uncertainty is normal when looking ahead. You might worry about failing, disappointing people, or missing God's plan. However, letting anxiety grow can block your progress.

- **Recognize Signs of Anxiety**: Trouble sleeping, constant worry, or feeling on edge can signal too much stress. Name these feelings instead of ignoring them.
- **Use Calm Strategies**: Deep breathing, short walks, or journaling prayers can help manage anxious moments.
- **Pray for Peace**: Philippians 4:6-7 urges believers to present their requests to God, promising peace that guards hearts. This includes worries about careers, finances, or relationships.
- **Take Small Steps**: Break big concerns into bite-sized actions. If you worry about selecting a college, start by researching a few local ones or scheduling a meeting with a guidance counselor.

Encouragement: God knows the future even when you do not. Trusting His care can transform worry into reliance, giving you calmness to face each day's tasks.

---

8. Developing Leadership Skills

Leadership is not just for people who want to run organizations. Leading can show up in everyday interactions—like guiding a project group at school or mentoring younger siblings. Strengthening leadership skills sets a strong foundation for adulthood.

- **Practice Communication**: Good leaders speak and listen well. Learn to articulate ideas clearly and understand others' viewpoints.
- **Take Initiative**: If a problem arises—like classmates confused about an assignment—step up to organize a study session.
- **Embrace Servanthood**: True Christian leadership often means serving, not bossing people around. Jesus washed His disciples' feet (John 13), showing humility and care.
- **Handle Criticism Kindly**: Leading draws opinions. Listen to constructive feedback, ignore unhelpful negativity, and keep improving.

Application: Whether you lead a youth group event or help your siblings complete chores, leadership is about guiding with empathy and responsibility. Over time, you can handle bigger responsibilities confidently.

---

9. Balancing Ambition with Humility

There is nothing wrong with aiming high. However, chasing personal glory can conflict with the biblical call to humility. Balancing ambition and humility helps you pursue excellence while staying grounded in God's truth.

- **Acknowledge God's Role**: Give thanks for your talents, opportunities, and achievements. Recognize they come from Him.
- **Avoid Boasting**: Share successes modestly. If people praise you, appreciate it, but redirect glory to God who made it possible.
- **Serve Others**: While pursuing your goals, remember to help those who might not have your advantages. This keeps your heart compassionate, not self-absorbed.
- **Stay Teachable**: No matter how skilled or smart you become, remain open to learning from peers, mentors, and even those younger than you.

Bible Connection: Micah 6:8 advises, "Do justice, love kindness, and walk humbly with your God." This verse captures the essence of a balanced approach to success.

---

10. Relying on Prayer and Scripture for Direction

Big decisions about the future can feel overwhelming if you rely solely on your own logic. Consistent prayer and biblical study give you a higher perspective.

- **Set Specific Prayer Times**: Whether it is a short prayer in the morning or at night, dedicate time to ask God for guidance in your goals and daily choices.
- **Search the Bible**: Look for verses related to your area of concern—like diligence, wisdom, or patience. Reflect on their relevance to your current decisions.
- **Listen Quietly**: Sometimes, you might sense a nudge or clarity after praying. It could be an idea, a verse that stands out, or confirmation through circumstances.
- **Seek Godly Counsel**: Share your prayer burdens with a trusted spiritual mentor. Ask them to pray with you for clarity about future plans.

Practical Tip: Keep a prayer journal. Write your questions about the future, note any Scriptures or advice you receive, and track how God responds over time.

---

11. Becoming Resilient Through Challenges

The path to a bright future is rarely smooth. You might face failures, setbacks, or closed doors. Resilience is key to bouncing back instead of giving up.

- **View Hardships as Lessons**: Each obstacle can reveal areas to improve, attitudes to shift, or better timing for your plans.
- **Seek Support**: Lean on friends, mentors, or family during tough moments. Sharing struggles can lighten your emotional load and bring solutions you had not considered.
- **Keep Perspective**: A single failure—like not getting into a certain club or missing a scholarship—does not define your life. God might have a different route for you.
- **Stay Flexible**: If one path closes, ask God to help you see new possibilities. Sometimes a pivot leads to better outcomes than your original plan.

Biblical Comfort: Romans 8:28 says that for those who love God, all things work together for good. Trusting this promise can sustain you when life feels unpredictable.

---

12. Serving While Pursuing Personal Goals

Pursuing a bright future does not mean focusing only on yourself. Integrating service keeps your ambition grounded in God's kingdom.

- **Volunteer Regularly**: If you plan to attend college, volunteering in a related area can boost your resume and help others. For instance, if you love medicine, volunteer at a clinic.
- **Mentor Younger Teens**: Show them study tips, share your experiences about faith challenges, or lead a small group at church.
- **Give Back**: If you succeed academically or financially, remember to support organizations or missions that serve the needy.
- **Inspire Peers**: Encourage your classmates also to keep faith in the mix when setting goals. Share your stories of how serving has refined your outlook.

Reflection: Jesus taught that whoever wants to be great should be a servant (Matthew 20:26). A future built on self-promotion can feel empty, but one filled with service to others aligns with Christ's example.

---

13. Preparing for Future Relationships and Family

While you are not necessarily planning marriage or parenthood yet, you can still cultivate habits that pave the way for healthy future relationships.

- **Emotional Maturity**: Learn to handle disagreements calmly and respect boundaries. This skill benefits friendships, family ties, and any eventual romantic partnership.
- **Purity and Respect**: Decide now what kind of dating boundaries you want, based on biblical guidelines. Think about how to treat a future spouse with love and loyalty.

- **Communication Skills**: Practice honesty, patience, and active listening in friendships. These traits form the backbone of good relationships later in life.
- **Teamwork**: Family life involves shared responsibilities. Knowing how to compromise and share tasks will help if you eventually live with a spouse or roommates in college.

Spiritual Insight: Ephesians 4:2-3 encourages humility, gentleness, patience, and unity. These virtues build strong relationships at every stage, whether it is with siblings or a future family.

14. Using Technology Responsibly for Future Goals

Technology can either help or hinder your progress. With the right approach, digital tools can be catalysts for learning, networking, and creativity.

- **Online Courses and Tutorials**: If you have a passion for coding, art, or languages, you can find free or affordable lessons online. These add to your skill set for future opportunities.
- **Networking**: Platforms like LinkedIn (if you are old enough) or school forums can connect you with professionals or classmates who share interests.
- **Building a Positive Online Presence**: Consider how your social media usage might affect college applications or job opportunities. Keeping posts respectful and mindful can leave a better impression.
- **Guarding Personal Time**: Set boundaries so you do not spend every free moment scrolling. Use digital tools to build your future, not to distract from it.

Hint: Some universities or employers might view your social media profiles. Presenting yourself with kindness, respect, and positivity aligns with Christian conduct and helps you stand out in a good way.

15. Building Lifelong Learning

Education does not end when you finish high school or college. Building a habit of ongoing learning can keep your mind sharp and broaden your understanding of the world.

- **Read Widely**: Explore different genres—biographies, Christian apologetics, history, and more. This enriches your perspective.
- **Stay Curious**: If you come across a concept you do not understand, research it. Curiosity leads to continuous improvement.
- **Attend Workshops**: Whether at church, school, or community centers, events on leadership, missions, or other skills can keep you informed.
- **Share Knowledge**: Teaching someone else what you learn reinforces your own grasp on the topic and benefits them too.

Spiritual Ties: Proverbs 1:5 mentions that a wise person seeks learning. Building a mindset of perpetual growth keeps you ready for whatever God calls you to do in your later years.

---

16. Keeping the Eternal Perspective

While planning for the future is wise, do not forget that earthly goals are temporary compared to eternity. Balancing earthly aspirations with a heavenly mindset prevents misplaced priorities.

- **Remember What Lasts**: Material success or recognition can fade. Faith, love, and relationships grounded in Christ endure forever.
- **Invest in People**: Your achievements can open doors, but how you treat others—showing God's love—has eternal implications.
- **Involve the Gospel**: Even if you become a doctor or a business owner, your true purpose includes sharing God's grace and living out Christian virtues.
- **Stay Humble**: Realize that, no matter how impressive your future accomplishments, your greatest identity is being a child of God.

Encouragement: Colossians 3:2 advises setting your mind on things above, not just on earthly matters. By doing so, you keep your future plans in proper perspective—important, but not ultimate.

---

17. Combating Fear of the Unknown

Fear about the future can paralyze you into indecision. But faith reminds us that God walks with us, no matter the unknown territory.

- **Name the Fear**: Are you worried about failing college exams? About not getting into your dream job? Once you identify the fear, you can face it directly.
- **Counter with Faith**: Recall biblical stories of how God guided people through uncertain times (like Abraham being called to leave his homeland).
- **Seek Mentors**: Talk with someone who overcame similar obstacles. Their story might dispel your fears and give you practical steps to move forward.
- **Action Over Avoidance**: Do not let fear freeze you. Taking small steps—like applying for a scholarship or seeking advice—breaks the grip of anxiety.

Biblical Perspective: Psalm 56:3-4 reminds us that when we are afraid, we can trust in God. Trust does not remove all unknowns, but it empowers you to proceed with courage.

---

18. Encouraging Others on Their Path

As you build your bright future, consider how you can also inspire friends or siblings. Collective encouragement fosters a more uplifting environment.

- **Share Resources**: If you find a helpful scholarship link or a good volunteer opportunity, pass it on to others.
- **Study Buddies**: If a classmate struggles, invite them to a study group. Mutual support leads to better results for everyone.
- **Cheer Achievements**: A friend who lands an internship or a sibling who improves their grades might appreciate a kind word from you.
- **Pray for One Another**: Knowing someone prays for your decisions, tests, or uncertain plans can infuse confidence and peace.

Rewarding Feeling: Helping others aim for a positive future strengthens your own sense of purpose and aligns with the Christian call to love our neighbors (Mark 12:31).

19. Looking Back to Appreciate Growth

While focusing on the future, do not forget to reflect on how far God has brought you already. Recognizing past growth fuels gratitude and confidence.

- **Recall Past Milestones**: Did you once struggle with a subject and now excel? Did you find new faith after a season of doubt? Look back and see God's work.
- **Learn from Past Errors**: If certain decisions led to trouble, use that knowledge to avoid repeating them.
- **Trace God's Hand**: Notice answered prayers or unexpected blessings. This record can strengthen you when new challenges arise.
- **Gratitude Journal**: Write down things you are thankful for weekly. Over time, you will see patterns of God's faithfulness that build hope for tomorrow.

Meaningful Truth: Regular reflection helps you see your life as a continuous story with God as the main author, guiding each chapter.

---

20. Moving Forward with Assurance

A bright future is not guaranteed by any formula, but you can move forward with assurance if you combine diligent planning, prayer, and trust in God. Your choices today—how you spend time, the habits you adopt, the people you bond with—create stepping stones for the years ahead. Even when unpredictability strikes, your faith remains an anchor, reminding you that the God who leads you day by day also holds every tomorrow.

Questions for Reflection

1. Which practical life skill could you start improving right now (cooking, budgeting, basic repairs)?
2. How do you see your current passions connecting to future career or service paths?
3. What steps can you take to keep an eternal mindset as you plan for immediate goals?

Practical Action Point
Choose one area related to your future—like financial awareness or career exploration—and commit to a concrete action this month. For example, if finances are your focus, start keeping a small budget notebook. If career exploration calls you, schedule a meeting with a school counselor or someone in the field that interests you. As you take this step, pray for clarity and trust God to guide each outcome.

Conclusion to Chapter 19
Your future holds many possibilities, and with God's guidance, you can prepare responsibly and with hope. Building solid habits—such as managing money, developing leadership, and strengthening personal values—lays the groundwork for the next stages of life. While you cannot predict every twist, you can remain confident that God's care extends to all your tomorrows. By blending biblical wisdom, prayer, and practical steps, you can look ahead with optimism, knowing each decision can reflect your commitment to honor God and serve others.

CHAPTER 20

Trusting God in All Areas of Life

Introduction
Trusting God sounds easy when everything goes smoothly. But real trust is tested during uncertainties, pain, or when we do not understand what is happening. For Christian teen girls, learning to trust God through every season—whether it is academic pressure, relationship drama, or personal doubts—can bring lasting peace. Trust does not eliminate hard times but anchors you so that hardships do not define or destroy you.

In this closing chapter, we will explore what it means to truly rely on God's wisdom and care. You will see how trust involves surrendering your fears, stepping out in faith, and believing that God is at work even in the most confusing circumstances. We will also look at ways to maintain trust over the long haul, using practical spiritual disciplines and a posture of humility. After finishing this chapter, you will have a roadmap to keep deepening your trust in God, no matter where life leads.

1. Understanding Real Trust in God

Trusting God goes beyond an intellectual belief that He exists. It means putting your reliance on Him daily—acknowledging that He knows best and is fully capable of handling your life details.

- **Dependence vs. Control**: If you try to manage everything on your own, you might push God's guidance aside. Real trust accepts that He can direct your steps more wisely than you can.
- **Active Choice**: Trust is not passive. You actively choose to lean on God's promises, especially when logic or emotions tempt you to doubt.
- **Rooted in Love**: You trust someone more when you know they love you. The Bible states that God loved the world so much He gave His Son (John 3:16). That is the ultimate expression of care.
- **Consistent Growth**: Trust develops through experiences with God—times you prayed and saw answers, or moments you felt peace despite chaos.

Encouragement: Psalm 37:5 says, "Commit your way to the Lord; trust in him, and he will act." This verse suggests that trusting is an active step—committing your path to God, expecting His involvement.

2. Trusting God with Your Emotions

Emotions can be wild. You might wake up feeling joyful, then shift to sadness by lunchtime. Trusting God means inviting Him into your emotional swings, not just your decisions.

- **Honesty in Prayer**: Instead of pretending your emotions are always positive, tell God if you feel angry, lonely, or afraid. He welcomes raw honesty (1 Peter 5:7).
- **Seeking Truth Above Feelings**: Emotions are real but not always factual. For example, feeling unloved does not mean you are unloved. Learn to match your feelings against God's truths in Scripture.
- **Asking for Healing**: Some emotions, like deep hurt or bitterness, need God's help to heal. Letting Him work in your heart can free you from grudges or despair.
- **Practicing Faith-Filled Responses**: When you feel anxious, remind yourself of God's promises. When you feel worthless, recall your identity as His beloved child.

Note: Jesus experienced strong emotions—He wept, felt compassion, and even expressed righteous anger. Yet He always brought those feelings before His Father, demonstrating that genuine trust includes emotional surrender.

---

3. Handling Unanswered Prayers

One big test of trust is when prayers go unanswered or God's timing seems slower than you prefer. It is tempting to assume He is ignoring you or does not care.

- **Remember God's Wisdom**: Sometimes, saying "no" or "wait" is part of God's better plan, even if it disappoints you initially.
- **Look for Growth**: Delayed answers can refine your patience, humility, or empathy. They can also teach you to keep praying persistently.
- **Stay Thankful**: You can still thank God for His presence and other blessings while waiting. Gratitude keeps your heart open rather than resentful.
- **Keep Praying**: Do not give up on communication with God. Persistent prayer can transform your perspective, even if the situation remains the same for a time.

Biblical Example: Paul prayed three times for a "thorn" to be removed from his life, but God did not remove it (2 Corinthians 12:7-9). Instead, Paul learned about God's grace being sufficient. This story shows that unanswered prayer can lead to deeper trust.

---

4. Trusting God in Relationships

From friendships to family bonds, relationships can bring joy or heartbreak. Trusting God means seeking His guidance in how you relate to people and handle conflict.

- **Seeking Wisdom for Conflict**: Pray before jumping into an argument. Ask God to help you speak truth calmly and listen well.
- **Dating or Friendship Boundaries**: Trusting God's design for healthy relationships might mean patiently waiting for the right timing or saying no to certain pressures.
- **Forgiving Others**: Biblical teaching on forgiveness (Matthew 6:14-15) challenges us. It is hard, but trusting God includes trusting that He calls us to show mercy for our own spiritual health as well as others'.
- **Relying on the Holy Spirit**: If you are unsure how to handle a tricky conversation, pray for the Spirit's guidance. He can give you words and attitudes beyond your natural abilities.

Outcome: Placing your friendships or romantic interests in God's hands can lead to deeper connections built on respect and shared faith, instead of fleeting emotional impulses.

---

5. Overcoming Fear of Failure

Sometimes, the fear of failing stops you from trying new things or stepping into responsibilities. Trusting God with your potential mistakes can free you to live more boldly.

- **Admit the Fear**: Trying to hide that you are scared keeps you stuck. Acknowledge it to God and maybe to a mentor.

- **Focus on Effort, Not Just Results**: You can control how much effort or preparation you put in, but the outcome sometimes depends on factors beyond your control.
- **Learn Through Failure**: If you do fail an exam or fall short in a performance, it is not the end of the world. Evaluate what went wrong, fix it next time, and keep going.
- **Remember God's Approval**: Your worth is not tied to achievements. Scripture says you are loved because you are His child, not because you performed perfectly.

Encouragement: The Bible shows many heroes who failed at points—Moses, Peter, Elijah—but God still used them mightily. Let their stories remind you that a setback does not disqualify you from God's plan.

---

6. Trust in Hard Times or Suffering

Pain, grief, or trials are a real part of life. Trusting God means holding onto Him even when you cannot see an immediate solution or sense His presence clearly.

- **Cry Out to God**: The Psalms show that you can pour out sorrow or confusion openly. God does not resent honest cries for help.
- **Seek Comfort in Scripture**: Verses like Psalm 34:18 ("The Lord is near to the brokenhearted") can soothe a hurting soul.
- **Use Support Systems**: Let friends, family, or church leaders pray for you or provide practical assistance. Suffering alone can intensify despair.
- **Look to Eternity**: In Romans 8:18, Paul talks about present sufferings not comparing to future glory. While that does not cancel current pain, it reminds you that hardship is temporary compared to eternal hope.

Deep Thought: Hard times can refine your faith. Fire purifies gold, and sometimes trials deepen your spiritual roots, revealing God's strength in your weakness.

---

7. Trusting God with Your Future Plans

We have discussed planning for the future, but trusting God is about laying those plans at His feet, believing He can open or close doors as He sees fit.

- **Surrender Your Dreams**: Tell God about your goals, then genuinely say, "Your will be done." If He redirects you, trust that He sees a bigger picture.
- **Take Action by Faith**: Trust does not mean waiting passively. Apply to schools, audition for programs, or pursue job opportunities while staying open to God's redirection.
- **Stay Flexible**: If a door you wanted remains shut, do not panic. Ask God for new paths or to show you what you might have missed.
- **Remember Past Guidance**: Look back at other times you thought you had a certain plan, but God led you differently—and it turned out better than you expected.

Biblical Example: In Acts 16, Paul tried to go into certain regions, but the Spirit prevented him. Later, he had a vision to go to Macedonia, which changed the spread of the gospel. This shows how God might redirect your course for a greater purpose.

---

8. Trusting God in Your Daily Routine

Sometimes, trust seems like a big concept for huge life events, but it also applies to daily routines—homework, chores, minor conflicts, or personal devotions.

- **Start the Day with Prayer**: Ask God to guide your interactions at school or home. Committing the day to Him invites His perspective into the mundane.
- **Pause for Small Decisions**: If you are tempted to talk back to a teacher or to skip a chore, trust God's principle of obedience and kindness. These small choices shape your character.
- **Thank God for Simple Blessings**: A meal, a sunny day, a good conversation—recognizing these gifts fosters a deeper trust that He cares about details.
- **Return to God in Stress**: A quick silent prayer during class or a chaotic moment at home can center you again on His presence.

Transformation: Embracing trust in daily tasks trains you to naturally lean on God in bigger challenges. Over time, trust becomes your default way of living.

9. Signs You Are Growing in Trust

How do you know if your trust in God is increasing? Look for these indicators:

1. **Less Anxiety**: You worry less about outcomes and more about faithful action.
2. **Greater Peace**: When problems arise, you might still feel concern but not a sense of panic, because you believe God is working.
3. **Obedience to Scripture**: Trusting God often manifests in obeying biblical commands, even if they are counter-cultural or uncomfortable.
4. **Resilience in Setbacks**: You bounce back faster after disappointment, confident that God remains in control.
5. **Desire for God's Will**: You genuinely want God's plan, not just your own preference.

Inward Joy: As trust grows, you might notice an underlying joy that remains even in adversity. This joy is rooted in confidence that God holds your life securely.

---

10. Overcoming Doubts and Distrust

Doubts can creep in when prayers feel unanswered or when you see suffering around you. A key part of trusting God is addressing those doubts openly.

- **Seek Clarification**: If you have theological questions, talk to pastors, read reputable Christian resources, and pray for enlightenment.
- **Observe God's Faithfulness**: Sometimes, journaling blessings or reflecting on testimonies of others can remind you of God's reliability.
- **Distinguish Distrust from Caution**: Some caution is wise (like verifying a new teaching). Distrust that leads to cynicism about God's character is harmful.
- **Refocus on Christ**: Jesus is the proof of God's love. When doubt clouds your view, meditating on the cross can reignite faith.

Encouragement: Even Jesus' disciples had moments of doubt (John 20:24-29). Jesus met them with grace, not condemnation. He can handle your doubts and lead you back to solid faith.

11. Trusting God When Facing Criticism or Persecution

Taking a stand for your Christian convictions can sometimes lead to mockery from peers or misunderstandings in secular environments. You might worry about being different or excluded.

- **Pray for Courage**: Boldness in the face of criticism often comes from praying like the early church did (Acts 4:29).
- **Stay Respectful**: Answer rudeness with gentleness and respect (1 Peter 3:15). Shouting back or insulting others does not show trust in God.
- **Know Your Identity**: If someone mocks your faith, remember who you belong to—God's family. Their opinions do not alter your identity in Christ.
- **Rely on God's Justice**: Sometimes, you cannot convince mockers to understand. Release the situation to God, trusting He sees all hearts and intentions.

Outcome: Standing firm in faith, even under ridicule, can deepen trust as you experience God's sustaining presence and the support of a Christian community.

---

12. Strengthening Trust Through Worship

Worship is not just singing; it is an attitude of honoring God. Expressing love and gratitude to Him can solidify trust, reminding you of His power and love.

- **Personal Worship**: Turn on worship music in your room, sing along, and think about the lyrics. Focus on God's attributes—His mercy, holiness, and majesty.
- **Corporate Worship**: Attending church and youth group gatherings helps you worship alongside other believers, which can encourage your own faith.
- **Gratitude in Prayer**: List the things you appreciate about God—His patience, kindness, the way He provides. This fosters a deeper sense of reliance.
- **Nature and Reflection**: Some find worship in nature, seeing God's handiwork. A quiet walk can become a worship moment if you connect creation back to the Creator.

Reflection: King David often praised God in Psalms, even when distressed. Praising God in tough times reaffirms your trust in His goodness over your circumstances.

---

13. Practical Steps to Deepen Trust

As you seek to trust God in all areas, simple disciplines can pave the way:

1. **Daily Devotion**: Even if it is 10-15 minutes, read Scripture and talk to God. Regular contact fosters familiarity with His voice.
2. **Bible Memorization**: Store God's promises in your mind. During unexpected challenges, these verses come back to guide you.
3. **Accountability**: Share your faith journey with a close friend or mentor. Ask them to encourage you when you doubt or slip.
4. **Act on Faith**: If you sense God nudging you to help someone or apologize for a wrong, do it promptly. Each step of obedience builds more trust.

Insight: Trust is like a muscle. The more you exercise it through daily choices—big or small—the stronger it grows.

---

14. Recognizing God's Work in Your Life

When God answers a prayer, provides a breakthrough, or grants peace in chaos, do not brush it off. Recognizing these moments cements your trust even more.

- **Testimonies**: Share with friends or youth leaders how God helped you pass a tough exam or solved a family issue. Hearing real stories of God's faithfulness encourages everyone.
- **Thankfulness Ritual**: Each week, write down at least one way you saw God at work. Over time, you will have a record of His goodness.
- **Avoid Pride**: Acknowledge God's hand, not just your own effort. This fosters humility and deeper reliance.
- **Keep Perspective**: Some answers might seem small, like finding a lost item. Others are huge, like healing from an illness. Both deserve gratitude.

Result: By regularly noting God's involvement, you reinforce the understanding that He is trustworthy, fueling even greater faith in days to come.

---

15. Trusting God with Your Identity and Worth

Many teen girls struggle with self-image or wonder if they are enough. Trusting God includes believing what He says about your value and uniqueness.

- **Rejecting Negative Messages**: The world may measure worth by looks, popularity, or achievements. Scripture says you are "fearfully and wonderfully made" (Psalm 139:14).
- **Recognizing God's Design**: Your personality, talents, and even quirks can serve His purpose. Trust that He formed you for a reason.
- **Combat Comparison**: When tempted to compare yourself to others, remember each person's path is different. God has a special plan tailored to you.
- **Affirmation Through Scripture**: Collect verses about God's love, such as Isaiah 43:1 where He calls you by name. Repeat them if insecurity arises.

Uplifting Result: Embracing your God-given identity fosters peace. You can chase goals confidently, not to prove your worth but to honor the One who created you with care.

---

16. Staying Faithful Over the Long Haul

Trust is not a one-time event; it is a lifelong posture. Seasons of life will shift—college, career, marriage, or other changes—but the call to trust God remains.

- **Stay in Community**: Whether you move away or stay local, find a church or fellowship that keeps you connected in faith.
- **Adapt Devotional Time**: Schedules will change, but maintain a routine of prayer and Bible reading, even if it looks different in each life stage.
- **Recall Past Faithfulness**: A habit of journaling answered prayers can guide you when you face new trials in adulthood.

- **Encourage Younger Believers**: You can pass on your stories of God's faithfulness to teens who come after you, just as older mentors once helped you.

Quiet Assurance: God remains constant (Hebrews 13:8). Even as your circumstances shift, you can continue to lean on Him as your unchanging foundation.

---

17. Overcoming Spiritual Dryness

Sometimes, you might feel distant from God—like your prayers bounce off the ceiling. This dryness can erode trust if you let it linger unchecked.

- **Evaluate Habits**: Are you neglecting prayer or skipping church? Sometimes dryness follows from drifting away from spiritual disciplines.
- **Confess Hidden Sins**: Guilt or unconfessed wrongdoing can block your sense of connection. Ask God's forgiveness and turn from destructive habits.
- **Seek Fresh Inspiration**: A new worship playlist, a Christian conference, or a different Bible reading plan can reignite your passion.
- **Wait and Rest**: Periods of dryness are normal in a faith journey. God can use them to teach perseverance and refine your motivations.

Comforting Thought: Even David, a man after God's heart, wrote psalms where he felt abandoned yet still ended in trust. Dry seasons do not mean God is absent; sometimes He is working in ways you cannot feel at the moment.

---

18. Surrendering Control Day by Day

Surrender is a big part of trust. It means loosening the grip on your life's steering wheel and letting God lead.

- **Symbolic Action**: Some people find it helpful to physically open their hands while praying, symbolizing giving God their burdens.
- **Daily Declarations**: Start the morning saying, "God, I trust You with my schedule, my interactions, my future. Guide me."

- **Letting Go of Perfectionism**: Trying to appear flawless can block you from leaning on God. Accept that His grace covers weaknesses.
- **Finding Peace**: Surrender often brings relief because you no longer feel the pressure to control every outcome.

Historical Example: Mary, the mother of Jesus, responded to the angel's message with, "I am the Lord's servant." She surrendered her reputation and future to God's plan, demonstrating deep trust.

---

19. Fruits of a Trusting Heart

When genuine trust in God becomes part of your lifestyle, it shows in how you carry yourself and interact with others.

- **Calm Confidence**: People might notice your stable presence during chaos, attributing it to some inner calm. That calm is rooted in trust.
- **Generosity**: Trusting God's provision frees you to give time, money, or encouragement to others without fear of running out.
- **Freedom from Others' Approval**: You are not enslaved to people's opinions because your security lies in God's love.
- **Authentic Joy**: Joy that persists in trials is a hallmark of someone who trusts God deeply. This joy can attract others to wonder about your source of peace.

Testimony: Your trust can become a witness to unbelievers, showcasing the difference God's presence makes in daily life. They might ask you about your secret to staying collected, offering you a chance to share your faith.

---

20. Final Encouragement: Walking Forward in Trust

Trusting God in every area—emotions, future, relationships, and hardships—forms the heartbeat of a vibrant Christian life. It does not guarantee a trouble-free existence, but it promises a peace that goes beyond circumstances. Even as you face unknown roads, burdens, and personal struggles, you can hold firmly to God's hand, assured that He directs your paths with love and wisdom.

Questions for Reflection

1. Which specific area of your life do you find hardest to trust God with right now?
2. What is one practical step you can take to surrender that area—like journaling a prayer or talking to a mentor?
3. How might trusting God more openly influence your friendships or family relationships?

Practical Action Point
Think of a current challenge—big or small. Each day for a week, take one minute to pray specifically about it, telling God you trust His outcome. Then, at the end of the week, note any changes in your feelings, perspective, or the situation itself. Reflect on whether consistent prayer has affected your level of trust.

Conclusion to Chapter 20
Trusting God in all areas of life may seem daunting, but it is the core of growing as a Christian. As you learn to lean on Him—bringing your anxieties, dreams, and daily tasks before Him—you cultivate a faith that stands firm in every season. This trust shapes your perspective on success, relationships, and even suffering. It calls you to daily surrender, confident that the One who formed you holds the future in His capable hands.

Final Thoughts on the Book

Over these twenty chapters, you have explored many facets of living as a Christian teen girl—understanding worth, building healthy friendships, forming positive habits, managing stress, and more. Each topic points back to the central truth: God is intimately involved in your life and cares about your growth. While you will face new challenges, joys, and responsibilities as the years go by, the principles here can guide you toward a solid, faith-anchored life.

May you continue to develop a deeper relationship with Christ, leaning on His Spirit for strength and wisdom. As you practice kindness, resilience, service, and trust, you become a light to others, reflecting God's love in practical ways. Remember that He is with you always, ready to walk alongside you through the simplest routines or the most significant crossroad decisions. Keep these truths close to your heart, and step forward with hope, courage, and unwavering trust in the God who never fails.

www.ingramcontent.com/pod-product-compliance
Lightning Source LLC
LaVergne TN
LVHW012042070526
838202LV00056B/5562